D0891463

THE CASE AGAINST FLOATING EXCHANGES

By the same author

Decline and Fall? Britain's Crisis in the Sixties

A Dynamic Theory of Forward Exchange

The Euro-Bond Market

The Euro-Dollar System

Foreign Exchange Crises

The History of Foreign Exchange

Leads and Lags: The Main Cause of Devaluation

A Textbook on Foreign Exchange

THE CASE AGAINST FLOATING EXCHANGES

PAUL EINZIG

MACMILLAN
ST MARTIN'S PRESS

First published 1970 by
MACMILLAN AND CO LTD
Little Essex Street London WC2
and also at Bombay Calcutta and Madras
Macmillan South Africa (Publishers) Pty Ltd Johannesburg
The Macmillan Company of Australia Pty Ltd Melbourne
The Macmillan Company of Canada Ltd Toronto
St Martin's Press Inc New York
Gill and Macmillan Ltd Dublin

Library of Congress catalog card no. 71–118572

SBN (boards) 333 10044 1

Printed in Great Britain by
R. & R. CLARK LTD
Edinburgh

Contents

Preface

THE object of this book is to discredit the case for 'gnomocracy' – a system under which the determination of exchange rates would be left to the mercy of speculators as a result of the adoption of floating exchanges. It is my contention that the theoretical arguments in favour of that system are utterly fallacious and that its supporters completely ignore the grave practical consequences of its adoption.

Until comparatively recently the agitation in favour of doing away with fixed exchange parities appeared to be a comparatively harmless if useless intellectual or pseudo-intellectual parlour-game. But during the last year or two the movement gained converts even in quarters which are liable to influence policy decisions. And the brief period during which the D. mark was allowed to float in 1969 gave fresh stimulus to the campaign for floating exchanges. Above all, President Nixon, in his message to Congress on 'United States Foreign Policy for the 1970s' came down emphatically on the side of those favouring more flexible exchanges, without specifying the degree and method of flexibility he would favour. The executive directors of the IMF are expected to submit to the annual meeting concrete proposals to reform the Bretton Woods system.

It has become all the more important, therefore, to re-examine the entire controversy of fixed versus floating exchanges. This must be done in a rational way, on the basis of the logic of inexorable facts, instead of relying on emotional appeals very similar to those made persistently by fanatic adherents of social credit over half a century. It is a strange spectacle to behold dignified and formerly orthodox theoretical economists and Central Bankers playing a role very similar to that formerly played by comic currency cranks.

My original reason for deciding to join in the controversy was the special study I had made of an aspect of the subject completely ignored or neglected both by advocates and by opponents of floating exchanges – the danger that under that system forward exchange facilities for importers and exporters would become inadequate to meet the greatly increased need for such facilities amidst wide and incalculable exchange fluctuations. Although in my earlier writings I sought to draw attention to the potential limitations to the volume of forward exchange facilities, owing to the technical character of this all-important point it played no part in the formulation of the case for and against floating exchanges.

The two opposing camps confined their arguments overwhelmingly to the theoretical sphere. My writings, which had meant to convey a warning on the basis of a practical conclusion derived from my lifelong study of forward exchange technique, were of course ignored in the course of discussions conducted in the rarefied atmosphere of pure theory. It was primarily in order to provide opponents of the proposal with fresh ammunition that I had decided to write the present book.

Not until I reached a comparatively advanced stage of my preliminary work on the book did I come to discover that there was also a fundamental fallacy in the theoretical case for floating exchanges, quite independently of my unanswerable practical argument against it. Accordingly I changed the plan of the book. Instead of fighting the case for floating exchanges entirely on technical grounds, I decided to attack its supporters in their own sphere and expose the fallacy in their theoretical argument.

It is my contention that advocates of the system are hopelessly mistaken in postulating that exchange rates, if allowed to take care of themselves without official interference, would float to a level at which imports and exports would automatically offset each other. The main object of this book is to prove that the rate at which supply and demand balance in the foreign exchange market is almost inevitably quite different from the rate at which imports and exports would balance. The whole case for floating exchanges rests on the false assumption that all transactions in the foreign exchange market are of commercial origin. Its supporters are guilty of overlooking the elementary fact that transactions originating through capital transfers, speculation and arbitrage always divert exchanges from the rate at which supply and demand derived from imports and exports would balance.

On the basis of long experience I have no illusions about my chances of being able to convert economists committed to the support of the case for flexibility. As for the possibility of converting ambitious opportunist politicians who favour floating exchanges because under that system they would be able to offer bigger and better bribes to the electorate, it may be assessed at nil. But I hope to reinforce opposition to the system with new arguments. And I hope to make those who are not committed to its support realise that those who are crusading for floating exchanges are trying to persuade the community to face grave risks on the basis of a false theory.

In spite of the overwhelming weight of the argument against floating exchanges, I envisage the possibility of its adoption in Britain and in other countries. If it should be adopted in any of the major industrial countries, I predict with the utmost assurance that the country concerned would follow in due course the example of Canada, France, Italy and other countries which, having experimented with that system, restabilised their currencies.

It seems probable that, for the present at any rate, some degree of common sense will prevail and the IMF will resist the growing pressure in favour of plunging the world into currency chaos by an early adoption of freely floating exchanges. The 'gnomocrats' – who believe in allowing speculators to rule our lives by determining the value of our currency – will have to wait a little longer before their dream becomes reality. But I am very much afraid that their day will come sooner or later. Mankind seems to have forgotten the lesson taught by inter-war experience in floating exchanges and will have to learn it all over again.

Meanwhile the IMF is likely to go a long way towards relaxing even the existing inadequate degree of discipline imposed on Governments and national economies by international monetary stability under the Bretton Woods system. At the time of writing the chances seem to be that before long the IMF will give its blessing to a moderate widening of the spread between the limits of permitted fluctuations. It will endorse a limited adoption of the 'crawling peg' even though that system would get the worst of every possible world. And it will authorise member-Governments to emulate the German experiment of 1969 in allowing their exchanges to float from their old parities to the new ones.

Perhaps it is not too much to hope that the disadvantages to be derived from meeting the 'gnomocrats' even half-way might bring the monetary authorities to their senses before they definitely commit themselves to the disastrous course towards which they are drifting.

Chapter 13, dealing with the limitations of forward exchange facilities under floating exchanges, is based largely on an article that appeared in the *Banca Nazionale del Lavoro Quarterly Review* of December 1968. In an Appendix entitled 'Why are U.K. Firms forbidden to Hedge?' – which first appeared in the form of an Aims of Industry Study – I draw attention to the way in which U.K. firms would be prevented under floating exchanges from safeguarding their vital interests against losses through exchange fluctuations. I should like to thank the two institutions for authorising me to reprint the material here.

The reader will find that in this book I have antagonised and insulted practically every one of its potential reviewers. I have even committed the equivalent of *lèse-majesté*, sacrilege and blasphemy combined, by criticising *The Economist*. I am only too well aware that by saying exactly what I think about the fanatical support of floating exchanges by my prospective critics I am virtually committing literary suicide. But I feel so strongly about it that I could not hope to die in peace if I had not said what I feel impelled to say, or if I had not said it in exactly the way I did.

P. E.

120 Clifford's Inn
London, E.C.4
February 1970

CHAPTER ONE

Introductory

THERE has always been a tendency on the part of writers on currency through the ages to conform to the prevailing fashions in respect of monetary theories and policies. Even allowing for this, the number of economists, financial editors and others writing or speaking about foreign exchange who in recent years joined the camp of advocates of floating exchanges is really amazing. So is the variety of reasons for which they have become convinced that it would be to the interests of Britain and of other advanced countries to abandon the stability of their exchanges. There is growing pressure on Governments, particularly from academic circles but also on the part of politicians of the irresponsible type, and by a large section of the Press, to allow the exchanges to float freely, or at any rate to adopt some system under which exchange rates would become much more flexible.

As we shall see in the next chapter, there is a widespread dissatisfaction in most countries, but especially in Britain and the United States, with the working of the Bretton Woods system of stable exchanges. Under that system the value of national currencies of countries associated with the International Monetary Fund is fixed in terms of dollars and of gold. The Governments of these countries are under obligation to keep exchange fluctuations within a permitted narrow range around the agreed parities. The rigidity of exchange rates under this system is becoming increasingly unpopular.

There is nothing new in this discontent with the existing system. There was hardly any prolonged period in the long history of foreign exchange during which there was no active and vocal discontent with the system in operation. Ever since the beginnings of the literature on foreign exchange we encounter from time to time strong agitation in favour of reforming the system of the day. Pressure for change became insistent during periods of currency crises, but would-be reformers were in evidence also during comparatively stable periods.

Some would-be reformers were dissatisfied because the exchanges were not stable enough, while others disliked the system because the exchanges were too stable. Changes were advocated because the existing system was considered to have handicapped the expansion of trade, or because stability of the exchanges failed to prevent instability of the domestic purchasing power of money, or because maintenance of stable exchanges drained the monetary resources needed for domestic requirements.

The unpopularity of the Bretton Woods system is discussed in Chapter 2. That system has come to be widely condemned because its rigid interpretation and application prevented, or at any rate delayed, adjustment of exchange parities called for by changes in the situation. The compulsory defence of stability has become increasingly unpopular because it has imposed on Governments and on national economies a degree of discipline that is incompatible with inflationary democracy. Demagogic demands for benefits that could only be attained with the aid of inflation have become an integral part of the democratic way of life.

The answer to that demand is sought in the creation of a system that would remove or greatly relax the economic and financial discipline imposed on countries which want to defend the stability of their currencies. Under the proposed system that is to take the place of Bretton Woods stability, exchanges would be allowed to depreciate freely, so that there would be no need for balancing Budgets, for restraining price or wage increases, or for other inconvenient measures necessitated by the defence of stable exchanges.

The reason why the idea of removing obstacles to inflation receives growing support lies in the inherently inflationary character of the democratic system, at any rate as it operates in Britain and in a number of other countries. Chapter 3 describes and indicts this misuse of democracy through competitive bidding for popularity by means of growing public spending and by abstaining from resisting wage inflation.

Although there are several possible alternatives to the Bretton Woods system, representing various degrees of flexibility, the most widely advocated system – advocated extensively in academic circles – is the system of freely floating exchange rates. Under floating exchanges, in their extreme form, parities would be abolished and gold would be demonetised. Exchange rates would be allowed to find their level free of official interference either in the form of maintaining support points to limit the fluctuations, or by applying exchange control, or by taking the initiative to intervene in the foreign exchange market in order to influence the trend of active exchange rates.

It is with this proposed system that the present book is mainly concerned, although it also deals with systems aiming at a less extreme degree of flexibility – floating sterling with systematic or occasional official intervention, frequent changes in fixed parities or support points, broadening of the band between maximum and minimum support points, the so-called 'crawling peg', and a mere reinterpretation of the Bretton Woods system so as to apply it in the sense in which it had been originally conceived by its authors – with changes of parities whenever there is fundamental disequilibrium.

The historical background to the flexible system is given in Chapter 4. Those who advocate a high degree of flexibility fancy themselves as bold radical reformers and even monetary revolutionaries. In reality the system they propose – or something more or less similar to it – has been actually in operation most of the time throughout the history of foreign exchange. Until after the Napoleonic Wars most exchanges were fluctuating most of the time within a more or less wide range. Apart from comparatively brief periods of relative stability, flexible and indeed floating exchanges had been in operation all the time in most countries. Even in more recent times it is easy to find instances of floating exchanges.

Chapter 5 seeks to ascertain the motives of those who have been advocating floating exchanges in recent years. It will be seen that, paradoxical as it may sound, the proposals originated both from monetary internationalism and from monetary nationalism. Some advocates of extreme flexibility claim to serve monetary internationalism by proposing a system under which, they contend, any form of restrictions on the free movement of goods and capital would become unnecessary. But others in favour of floating rates try to serve, purposely or otherwise, the diametrically opposite end, that of isolationist monetary and economic nationalism. They recommend floating rates as a means of enabling their country to pursue economic and social policies independently of those pursued by other countries, and to the detriment of other countries. They want it in order to be free to adopt concealed export bounties and import restrictions in the form of currency depreciation. Some advocates of the system are idealist dogmatists, while others are self-seeking demagogues who want to outbid their political rivals – whether in opposite parties or in their own parties – by removing the obstacles to their ability to offer bigger and better bribes to the electorate.

The economic theory that lies behind the advocacy of the monetary policy of floating exchanges is described and analysed in Chapter 6. It will be seen that many academic supporters of the system are in its favour because they firmly believe that exchange rates, left to themselves, would tend to settle down around an 'equilibrium level' – a level at which imports and exports would tend to balance. It is one of the main objects of this book to discredit this theory and to expose its utterly fallacious character. I shall try to prove that the supposed existence of such an equilibrium level of exchange rates is a myth. Those who believe or profess to believe in its existence overlook or disregard the self-aggravating character of exchange movements and the variety of conflicting influences that are liable to divert exchange rates from their equilibrium level for the purposes of foreign trade. They are oblivious of the elementary fact that supply and demand in the foreign exchange market depend not only on foreign trade transactions but also on foreign exchange transactions of other kinds.

The self-aggravating character of exchange movements is further analysed in the next four chapters. Chapter 7 argues that even if the foreign exchange market were confined to transactions arising from imports and exports only, it would be quite inconceivable for exchange rates to settle at the level at which the supply and demand originating from trade would necessarily balance. A wide variety of incalculable elasticities influence the effect of changes in exchange rates on the volume and value of imports and exports, effects which, unless they happen to cancel each other out, would divert exchange rates from their trade equilibrium level. Their effect on the terms of trade is anybody's guess. Those who believe in the existence of a rate at which a trade deficit is bound to disappear overlook the possibility of self-aggravating exchange movements, such as were witnessed on innumerable occasions ever since the First World War. Some of the crusaders for floating exchanges carry their dogmatism even further by declaring their faith in the possibility that floating rates would reach an equilibrium level at which not only are imports and exports balanced, but balanced at full employment.

This belief in the existence of an equilibrium rate is based on a static theory which overlooks the fact that exchange rates, by deviating from their equilibrium levels for no matter what reason, tend to change the equilibrium levels themselves. As a result of this basic tendency, deviations from equilibrium level do not result in mere temporary discrepancies but tend to create new equilibrium levels. The reciprocal character of the relationship between exchange rates and their trade equilibrium levels is overlooked by advocates of floating exchanges.

Chapter 8 examines one of the major influences that is liable to cause self-perpetuating deviations from the original equilibrium level – international capital movements. Their disturbing effect is superimposed over the self-aggravating tendencies within the trade factor dealt with in the previous chapter. Even if there existed a level at which foreign exchange transactions arising from international movements of capital would tend to balance, it would be quite different from trade equilibrium level. There may be an equilibrium level for movements of short-term funds which are largely independent of imports and exports of goods and services. But it is highly doubtful whether movements of long-term capital have any equilibrium level at all. The import and export of capital is liable to be affected by a set of influences totally independent of those affecting trade. It would be sheer coincidence if trade and capital movements came to be balanced at the same exchange rate. For one thing, even in normal conditions, capital movements depend on interest rates rather than on exchange rates.

Another factor causing deviations of exchange rates from their trade equilibrium level is speculation, dealt with in Chapter 9. Although there can be speculation in a balancing sense, as likely as not it tends to be unbalancing. Speculation is affected by a multitude of influences besides the trade balance and its effect on exchange rates. Speculative buying and selling of exchanges are liable to offset each other at exchange rates that differ considerably from the rate at which imports and exports tend to offset each other. The resulting discrepancies might delay the adjustment of the floating rate to its trade equilibrium level, or they might make it overshoot that level.

Chapter 10 aims at breaking new ground by discussing the unbalancing effect of various types of arbitrage. Although arbitrage, by offsetting discrepancies, is assumed to be an equilibrating influence, it is quite capable of generating or aggravating disturbing dynamic effects.

The findings contained in Chapters 7 to 10 are summed up in Chapter 11, which sets out the reasons why exchange movements under the floating system could not be relied upon for automatically balancing imports and exports. A balance of payments deficit can not be wiped out by the simple device of allowing the exchange rate to float down to its trade equilibrium level.

Chapter 12 explains why the system of floating rates would stand less chance of producing tolerable results today than it had before the war. The background against which it would operate would be totally different from pre-war conditions, when there was large unused productive capacity and labour was less inflexible. Stress is laid on the asymmetric character of the system in present-day conditions, when wages and prices respond very readily to depreciations but not to appreciations of the fluctuating exchanges.

Chapter 13 is of crucial importance. It explains why and how the volume of forward exchange facilities available for importers and exporters would tend to contract sharply under floating exchanges, while the need for such facilities for covering the increased exchange risk would increase. Should importers and exporters be unable to obtain covering facilities, except at prohibitive costs, many of them would prefer to abandon the transactions rather than expose themselves to ruinous losses. The resulting contraction of world trade might trigger off a world-wide slump with incalculable consequences.

Having examined the economic consequences of the most extreme form of 'gnomocracy', the book proceeds to discuss more restrained forms of flexibility. Chapter 14 discusses the possibility of floating rates between currency areas, concluding that it combines the advantages of stability within the limited sphere of currency areas with the disadvantages of instability in relation to countries outside the areas.

Some supporters of the system of floating rates concede that it might be expedient to moderate the fluctuations resulting from the adoption of that system by means of various forms of official intervention. Chapter 15 points out that, while it might be possible to reduce the disadvantages of uncontrolled fluctuations by means of intervention, this would tend to produce the very same effects which the opponents of stable parities would like to eliminate through the adoption of floating exchanges. The same is true concerning the system of 'managed flexibility', discussed in Chapter 16, under which fixed parities would be retained but the peg would be changed very frequently.

Two widely-canvassed gimmicks, the 'band' proposal and the 'crawling peg', are dissected in Chapters 17 and 18. Both proposals – the broadening of the spread between support points which limit the fluctuations of exchange rates around their fixed parities, and the replacement of infrequent major changes in parities by weekly or monthly fractional changes – constitute a compromise between stable and floating exchanges. They are put forward in the hope of being able to enlist the support of those who are afraid of extreme flexibility but might be willing to accept a formula which might be developed in due course into a system of more or less freely floating exchanges.

Chapter 19 examines the possibilities and difficulties of improving the existing system of stable parities by applying it in the spirit in which the Bretton Woods plan was conceived by its authors. It allows for a fairly high degree of flexibility, but in practice the Governments of advanced countries are unwilling to change their parities even in circumstances when they would be in a position to do so under the rules of the IMF. The conclusion is that the existing system could and should be applied less rigidly without yielding to the temptation of taking the line of least resistance whenever changes of parities appear to be a more comfortable solution than alternative ways of dealing with a disequilibrium.

The concluding chapter examines the question whether temporary adoption of floating exchanges for the limited purpose of adjusting parities would not be doing the right thing in the wrong way. There is a strong case for major changes of parities, and there is indeed a particularly strong case for a substantial increase in the gold value of the dollar. But the Governments concerned are reluctant to face the unpopularity of making the change and might prefer to let the foreign exchange market determine the new parities. This was what happened with the D. mark in September and October 1969, even though the authorities felt impelled to intervene in order to reinforce the upward trend of the exchange. Evidently, unregulated market trends cannot be relied upon for producing the right rate. As an experiment in floating exchanges adopted to that end, the German experiment was a failure and did not justify the enthusiasm with which it was welcomed by advocates of floating exchanges.

Nevertheless quite conceivably much-needed adjustments of parities would only be politically practicable in the untidy way of allowing the rates to float. But it is very much open to question whether the favourable final results are worth the risk involved in the method by which they are sought to be achieved, and whether it would not be wiser to do the right thing in the right way.

Unfortunately there seems to be more than an even chance that the wrong thing will be done in the wrong way. As a reaction to undue rigidity, the free world is likely to relapse into undue flexibility in some form, quite possibly in its extreme form of floating exchanges. Had that system been adopted at the end of the war, in all probability the pound would be worth considerably less than a shilling by now. For neither Conservative nor Socialist Governments would have prevented its depreciation. And if anyone is tempted to support the adoption of floating exchange rates in the near future, he would have to reckon with a fall in the value of the pound to less than a shilling, compared with its present depreciated value, by the end of the 'seventies.

Even if the de-stabilisation of sterling should be well timed so that it would be played from strength and sterling would float or crawl upward to begin with, the turn of its trend would be only a question of time. Having abandoned the principle of its stability, its downward floating or crawling would not be resisted and would soon gather momentum. There could be no doubt about the ultimate outcome.

CHAPTER TWO

Why Stability is Unpopular

STABILITY of exchange, achieved and, on the whole, maintained under the Bretton Woods system, is becoming increasingly unpopular – even more so than stability under the gold standard had been. Opposition to it is becoming increasingly vocal and militant, and some of it comes from quite unexpected academic quarters. The general public, without being able to follow the intricacies of the technical and often deliberately obscurantist arguments involved, seems to be yielding gradually to the hypnotic effects of frequently repeated demagogic slogans in favour of flexible exchanges.

Politicians, too, are advocating it and appear to think they are on a good wicket. Quite possibly they are from the point of view of their personal prospects, if not from that of their country's vital interests. It would not be altogether surprising if the nineteenth-century American electioneering slogan, 'You shall not crucify mankind on a cross of gold', reappeared at some election in the near future in a form adapted to present-day conditions – and with a different result – unless the Bretton Woods system of monetary stability, which is now presented as the successor of W. J. Bryan's 'cross of gold', is abandoned even before it is submitted to the verdict of the electorate in one of the leading countries.

There must have been widespread dissatisfaction most of the time with the monetary system of the day, ever since that institution came into being. When collecting material for my books *Monetary Reform in Theory and Practice*, *Primitive Money in its Ethnological, Historical and Economic Aspects*, and *The History of Foreign Exchange*, I came across many early instances of such dissatisfaction, albeit prevailing in totally different circumstances from those prevailing in our days.

Of course the lay public is always inclined to regard money – not only in the concrete sense of the term but also as a meaningless or meaningful symbol and as an abstract system – as 'the root of all evil'. In many past periods experts and pseudo-experts endeavoured to persuade Governments, Parliaments and the people to remedy the deficiencies of money, deficiencies which some would-be reformers had denounced with a crusading zeal amounting at times to a fanaticism comparable to that displayed today by advocates of floating exchanges. Beginning with Plato, who wanted to do away with money altogether for domestic purposes, and ending with our 'gnomocrats', there have been such would-be monetary reformers in good times as well as in bad times. One only has to recall the perennial agitation against the gold standard towards the end of the last century – even though in retrospect the period of its operation now appears to many people as the golden age of stability – first by bimetallists and later by monetary expansionists of all descriptions, to show that there is nothing out of the ordinary in the present unpopularity of the Bretton Woods system of stable exchanges.

It would of course be idle to deny that Bretton Woods stability has its disadvantages, just as there had been another side to stability under the gold standard. But while agitation against the gold standard had been confined most of the time to currency cranks – at any rate until the 'twenties, when radical reformers of the standing of Keynes and McKenna raised it to a higher intellectual level – much of the opposition to the system of stability in our own days comes very largely from highly respectable orthodox and near-orthodox circles.

Until 1931, 99 per cent of the economists and bankers were either actively in favour of maintaining the stability of exchanges achieved through the operation of the gold standard, or they took it simply for granted. Today the large majority of academic economists and even some bankers – including some Central Bankers – Treasury officials and, of course, politicians, are in favour of abandoning the stable conditions that have been maintained under the Bretton Woods system.

That system was established immediately after the Second World War, under the influence of war-time fears of a recurrence of the currency chaos that followed the First World War and came to be revived in the 'thirties. The experts who had negotiated the Bretton Woods Agreement, and the Governments that had endorsed it, had been inspired by a desire to learn from the lessons of inter-war experience and to prevent its recurrence after the removal of war-time exchange controls. To that end even Keynes changed his earlier opposition to exchange stability. He was also willing to abandon the 'Keynes Plan' – proposals to provide for a wider scope for monetary expansion than could be provided through the adoption of the White Plan. After prolonged rearguard action Keynes accepted the substance of the much less expansionary American formula which was to become the basis of the Bretton Woods Agreement, but not without securing the insertion of provisions to ensure that the new system should not be as rigidly restrictive as the gold standard had been.

Opponents of the Bretton Woods Agreement – I must confess I was one of them during 1944–46 – failed to appreciate, and many of them still fail to appreciate, the full extent of the progress towards expansionism and flexibility it represented compared with the gold standard and even compared with the gold exchange standard. All the potential means of expansion that had existed under the latter remained, and the increasing facilities provided by the International Monetary Fund provided additional scope for expansion. Moreover, there were escape clauses to ensure the possibility of a much greater flexibility for exchange parities than they had had under the gold standard.

Resistance to the adoption of the system that was to be established under the Bretton Woods Agreement had been tempered by the memories of the currency chaos experienced under the system of floating exchanges in the 'twenties and 'thirties. The system that had promised to prolong war-time stability of exchange rates was welcomed with open arms by most people. Those of us who would have preferred to return to flexibility had been influenced by pre-war experience, when flexibility enabled Britain to defend her economy against imported deflation. Quite wrongly we had assumed that wartime inflation would be followed by a slump and by a severe prolonged depression, just as it had during the years after the first World War. To prevent that, we should have liked to return to flexible exchanges, a system that seemed to have served Britain well in the 'thirties, having obviated the necessity of deflating in order to keep pace with deflation abroad.

Keynes had shared these fears. While Britain's weak bargaining position prevented him from rejecting the White Plan aiming at curtailing her freedom to devalue, during the prolonged negotiations he successfully insisted on the insertion of safeguards against an undue rigidity of the agreed parities.

The maximum between the limits of permitted fluctuations around the parities was fixed at 2 per cent – 1 per cent on each side of the parities – which was somewhat wider than the spread between gold import points and gold export points under the gold standard before 1914 and during 1925–31. Keynes himself suggested before the war a widening of the spread to 2 per cent.

But in practice most leading member countries of the IMF did not avail themselves in full of even this modest concession to flexibility. They fixed their maximum and minimum support points in relation to the dollar at about $\frac{3}{4}$ per cent on each side of their parities with the dollar, making a spread of $1\frac{1}{2}$ per cent in all, and a spread of about 3 per cent for exchange rates between currencies other than the dollar.

A much more important concession to flexibility was the rule under which member countries were authorised to change their parities by 10 per cent in either direction without having to obtain authorisation from the IMF. Any more substantial devaluations or revaluations were subject to authorisation by the IMF. But it was part of the rules that devaluations would be authorised in case of 'fundamental disequilibrium'. The meaning of fundamental disequilibrium was not defined clearly.

In fact it was left deliberately vague in the Bretton Woods Agreement and in subsequent interpretations and amendments of its rules.

What mattered was that the IMF was given the power to object to devaluations in excess of 10 per cent. In theory the Bretton Woods system appeared to have introduced a high degree of rigidity of exchange rates. Even though it admitted the broad principle that in cases of one-sided pressure due to fundamental disequilibrium the countries concerned should be permitted to change their parities, the interpretation of that principle was left to the IMF, a body which was largely controlled by the United States Government, the chief opponent of flexibility. This explains the hostility of expansionists to the system, which was denounced in and out of season as an obstacle to economic growth.

In practice, however, member Governments could easily have disregarded the limitations imposed on changes of parities, had they wished to do so. Since discussions over applications to the IMF by member countries for authorisation to devalue are always conducted behind closed doors, there is no means of knowing how many applications, if any, were rejected, or in how many instances was the extent of permitted devaluations scaled down. What we do know is that up to the beginning of 1969 member countries devalued on more than two hundred occasions, and on none of these instances was there any objection voiced in public by the IMF. The number of unopposed devaluations by leading industrial countries was eight. To this number another was added in 1969 – the devaluation of the French franc, for which no authorisation was asked from the IMF.

It seems safe to assume that even if the IMF objected to devaluations or to their extent, any Government that felt strongly about the need for devaluing would be in a position simply to disregard these objections. In theory the possibility of refusing to grant further financial support by the IMF is supposed to be an effective deterrent. In practice there are several reasons why the Government that wishes to devalue in disregard of the veto of the IMF would be in a position to do so. First of all, such a decision is not likely to be taken by any Government unless the country concerned has already reached or approached the limits of its drawing facilities with the IMF. Having incurred substantial liabilities to the IMF, it was to the interest of the latter to enable its debtor to remain or to become solvent in order to be able to meet its liability. Continued defence of its currency at an overvalued parity would be against the interests of the IMF in its capacity as creditor. In any case, the immediate effect of a devaluation of an overvalued currency would be wholesale coverings of short positions in that currency, a return of hot moneys withdrawn before devaluation, and later some improvement in the balance of payments. For some time at any rate after an unauthorised devaluation the offending country would not require any new assistance from the IMF.

It is true, as experience has proved again and again, that during periods of inflation devaluations seldom solve the problem of countries resorting to them too easily, except quite temporarily. So Governments might feel deterred from disregarding the veto of the IMF by their fear that the latter might be reluctant to come to their aid on the next occasion when its aid would be required once more. But some Governments are not sufficiently far-sighted to worry unduly about tomorrow's problems, so long as they think they can solve today's problems by devaluing regardless of the attitude of the IMF.

Over and above all, offending Governments may feel justified in assuming – probably rightly – that, in spite of their bad behaviour, the IMF would be anxious to help them to avoid yet another devaluation of their currencies. This is particularly true of important currencies, the devaluation of which would be liable to produce extensive chain-reactions in the international monetary sphere. The chances are that the IMF would grant assistance to such countries regardless of their past records.

The fact that countries in difficulties are in a strong bargaining position in relation to the IMF is indicated by the extent to which the IMF authorised a number of member countries to disregard its basic rules. It raised no public objection to the adoption of floating exchanges by France, Italy, Canada and other member countries during the 'fifties. Multiple currency practices were not outlawed, and in many instances even exchange restrictions were tolerated and their early removal not insisted upon too firmly.

Discipline imposed on member Governments by the IMF was not the main reason why member countries, the currencies of which came under pressure, did not devalue more frequently, or why they did not allow their exchanges to float downwards. Opponents of the Bretton Woods system keep repeating to boredom that Britain was, and still is, prevented by her adherence to the IMF and acceptance of its rules from expanding her economy more rapidly. In reality, the reason why sterling was only devalued twice since the war was simply the British Government's unwillingness to devalue more often. Had Britain or other countries wanted to do so, the rules of the IMF would have been powerless to prevent them in practice. The IMF could not even have denounced in public the countries concerned for dishonouring their undertaking. Any such publicity would have been highly damaging and might have aggravated the situation of the countries concerned, or it might have deprived them of the favourable initial psychological effects of the unauthorised devaluations. Clearly this would not have helped the IMF in any way. Hence the alacrity with which the IMF endorsed the unauthorised French devaluation in 1969.

In any case there is no reason to believe that it is the policy of the IMF to resist too firmly, if at all, applications for authorisations to devalue, if the currency concerned is obviously under strong adverse pressure. Quite the contrary, there is reason to believe that in 1949 the IMF actually urged the British Government to devalue sterling. At any rate there is known to have been pressure to that end on the part of the United States Treasury, and since American influence was predominant in the IMF it is safe to assume that pressure exerted by the IMF on Britain was on that occasion in favour of devaluation and not against it. Nor is there any reason to suppose that when in 1967 the British Government devalued sterling once more she did so in defiance of objections by the IMF, although possibly the IMF exerted its influence to dissuade Britain from a heavier devaluation.

The way in which the Bretton Woods system tends to discourage devaluations is not through any rigid application of its letter but through its spirit. There was no international agreement or international institution in the 'thirties which would have been in a position to prevent or discourage devaluations or suspensions of the gold standard. Such acts were regarded since time immemorial as the sovereign right of any independent State. Nevertheless, countries of high standing always considered it beneath their dignity to exercise that right and did the utmost to avoid doing so. There were no suspensions of the gold standard or devaluations unless the Governments concerned came to the conclusion that it was no longer possible to resist adverse pressure on their currency.

Under the Bretton Woods system, too, it was not the signature of member Governments on the relevant treaties, or such veto as may be exercised in theory by the IMF, that prevented Britain from devaluing sterling each time it came under strong adverse pressure. It was the spirit of the system, under which it would have been undignified to allow any currency of high standing to depreciate beyond its agreed support point. Any devaluation would have been considered both at home and by world opinion as an admission of defeat, as indeed were the devaluations of 1949 and 1967. This consideration of prestige and dignity was a more effective deterrent to unauthorised devaluations, or even to authorised devaluations, than the rules of the IMF.

This rigid resistance to devaluations in the face of strong and persistent pressure is not in accordance with the intentions of the authors of the Bretton Woods Agreement or the founders of the IMF. They clearly envisaged changes of parities whenever fundamental disequilibrium developed. From this point of view the Governments of the leading countries have been most of the time more royalist than the king. They have imposed on themselves a degree of self-discipline that is stricter than the discipline imposed on them by the letter of the Bretton Woods system. On a number of occasions they resisted changes in parities in situations when such changes would have been in accordance with both the letter and the spirit of the Bretton Woods Agreement and with the rules of the IMF. Unfortunately their resistance often assumed the form of using up their reserves and incurring foreign debts in a stubborn defence of parities against the effects of a disequilibrium of the balance of payments, instead of fighting the adverse trend by adopting measures to restore equilibrium.

In any case, critics of the Bretton Woods system ought to be reminded that the proof of the pudding is in the eating. While before the war the basic trend of the economy had been deflationary, since its adoption the free world witnessed almost uninterrupted creeping inflation. Recessions occurred from time to time, but they were mild and there was no return to mass-unemployment. There was more economic progress during the past two decades than during any similar period in economic history, in spite of Bretton Woods – or perhaps largely because of Bretton Woods.

CHAPTER THREE

Democracy Tempered by Inflation

WE saw in the last chapter that the system of stable exchanges is now subject to much more criticism than there had been under the gold standard. The main reason for the growing pressure in favour of more flexible exchange rates lies in the degeneration of democracy into demagogy. In my book *The Control of the Purse: Progress and Decline of Parliament's Financial Control*, I dealt with eighteenth-century political corruption under a chapter heading of 'Democracy Tempered by Corruption'. I tried to indicate the extent to which, and the ways in which, democracy, which had emerged victorious in Britain as a result of the bloodless revolution of 1688, was debased through the wholesale buying of votes at elections by politicians and political parties, and through the buying of politicians' votes in Parliament by the Governments of the day.

Under ideal democracy the votes should go in favour of those whose policies appear to serve the public interest to a higher degree than those of their opponents. The democracy in Britain during the eighteenth century was 'tempered', however, by the possibility of influencing decisions through offering financial advantages to the electors, and the willingness of Members to sell their votes in return for lucrative offices or other benefits. But the scale of political bribery two centuries ago, notorious as it may now appear to most historians, was moderate compared with what it is in our time. Indeed in 1713 the House of Commons passed a 'self-denying ordinance' under which the right to initiate public expenditure was relinquished in favour of the Crown. Members deprived themselves of the opportunity to reward their supporters by taking the initiative for allocating public money in ways beneficial to influential constituents.

Nevertheless, politicians of the eighteenth century had earned an unenviable reputation for corruption. Yet political corruption two centuries ago was negligible compared with present-day political corruption. Our contemporary politicians bribe the electorate on an infinitely vaster scale, though in less crude and obvious ways. Unlike their forerunners of 1713, they have not relinquished their privileges of bribery by inflation or by promises which could only be implemented by inflation. Hence the heading of the present chapter, implying that idealistic democracy in this country – and in other democratic countries in a similar position – is 'tempered' by political bribery causing or accentuating inflation. Although the Government of the day still retains the initiative for wholesale bribery, it is backed by the rank and file's endorsing inflationary policies producing that effect.

Progress of the democratic trend since the Second World War manifested itself partly in the adoption of the Welfare State and in giving high priority to policies aiming at the achievement and maintenance of full employment. Both full employment and the Welfare State are ideals for the sake of which it is well worth our while to submit to the disadvantages arising from their inherently inflationary character. But competitive political bribery by rival political parties has unjustifiably increased the extent of their inflationary effect. This argument is developed in fuller detail in my *Decline and Fall? Britain's Crisis in the Sixties*. Here let it suffice to say that the way in which politicians had presented, and are still presenting, these major concessions to the working classes, as a free gift from Santa Claus which need not be deserved and earned through hard and honest work, has generated a wrong attitude on the part of those who benefit by full employment and by the Welfare State. Although my findings were based entirely on recent British experiences, other democratic countries, too, had similar experience, even though to a smaller degree in most countries.

The Welfare State is inherently inflationary because it calls for heavy increases in public spending and results in a more egalitarian distribution of incomes. But politicians of both parties have made them more inflationary than would have been necessary. Oppositions since the war have created a political atmosphere amidst which the maintenance and further development of inflationary policies has come to be regarded as an absolute political necessity. The *quid pro quo* that is expected of the beneficiaries consists, not of hard and honest work, but of votes for the party that offers bigger bribes. In this respect, however, politicians are often disappointed because the British electorate – like judges in a certain country – accepts the bribes from both parties and delivers judgement according to its conscience. Which experience does not deter politicians from trying again and again to buy votes by making inflation when in office and by promising inflation when out of office.

In the demoralising atmosphere created by politicians, the Welfare State and the maintenance of a high level of employment tend to cause an unnecessarily high degree of cost inflation and demand inflation. By presenting full employment as a birthright for the working classes instead of presenting it as a concession which must be earned and deserved, full employment came to produce the maximum of disadvantages in the form of unearned wages and the minimum of benefits for the community in the form of higher output.

The wrong spirit in which the Welfare State had been adopted and is applied has unnecessarily increased its inflationary costs and has prevented the development of a spirit in which the benefits received would provide an incentive to earn their cost by hard and honest work. No politician has the courage to tell the beneficiaries that increased social service benefits are not the free gift of the Government in office or of the Opposition pressing for their increase, but the gift of the community which must be reciprocated by helping the community to earn their costs.

It would have been possible to keep down the inflationary

effect of the Welfare State through harder work by the beneficiaries and potential beneficiaries, and by abstaining from abusing the favours conferred on them. Instead, the Welfare State and overfull employment in Britain have created a spirit in which most people have been trying to get the maximum of free services out of the community in return for giving the minimum of services to the community. The net result was additional purchasing power unaccompanied by additional goods.

The resulting cost and demand inflation inevitably reacts on the balance of payments and on exchanges. Effective measures in support of the exchanges forced Governments to make occasional minor cuts in Welfare State expenditure and to delay its increase. From time to time they reduced the degree of employment, or at any rate mitigated the degree of overfull employment.

Major cuts in excessive consumer spending, enforced in order to reduce the adverse balance of payments, are necessarily detrimental to the objectives of the Welfare State and to full employment. And since, in accordance with the spirit of the Bretton Woods system, Governments have to defend their exchanges before they take the line of least resistance by devaluing, their defensive measures adopted to that and have prevented full employment and the Welfare State from producing their full beneficial effects.

It is entirely wrong to contend that the degree of stability of exchanges established under the Bretton Woods system is inimical to the basic interests of full employment and of the Welfare State. After all, the experience of nearly a quarter of a century proves that the requirements of stable exchanges do not prevent the development, maintenance and extension of the Welfare State and do not lead to any large-scale unemployment. Quite the contrary, under Bretton Woods stability social service benefits have risen to a level undreamt of during the inter-war period of floating exchanges. Stability had not prevented the increase in employment, and unemployment had virtually disappeared. Although it rose slightly in Britain as the effect of disinflationary measures in 1967–69, even during that period the number of registered *and unregistered* vacancies always exceeded the number of genuine unemployed who were willing to accept jobs outside their own industry and outside the area of their residence.

It is of course always arguable that without Bretton Woods stability it might have been possible to distribute even more generous social service benefits, and the number of unemployed in Britain – which is around 600,000 at the time of writing – might have been kept down at 250,000, which represents more or less the number of unemployables, those in transit between jobs, and those seasonally unemployed. But this argument overlooks the dangers that the resulting acceleration of the increase in consumer demand, in wages and in prices, in the absence of its interruptions by the 'stop–go–stop' policy, might have culminated in an inflationary boom leading to a slump and a prolonged depression. Or it might have culminated in uncontrollable, self-aggravating runaway inflation.

Opponents of Bretton Woods stability fail to appreciate that, for the first time in modern history, the world has been free of a major slump for something like a quarter of a century, not counting the war years. This was the result of the system of 'stop–go' under which Governments sought to check inflationary trends before they got out of control. The reason why policies aiming at stability have not been even more effective is that, for fear of the political unpopularity of measures to interrupt inflation, in Britain and some other countries such measures were not adopted soon enough or to a sufficient degree. In Britain they were always 'too little and too late'. Their delay and their inadequacy made it necessary to adopt harsher and even more unpopular measures later. But it is wrong to blame the Bretton Woods system for the hardships caused by such drastic measures, because they could and should have been mitigated, if not avoided, by resorting to earlier and more effective measures.

Admittedly, under flexible exchanges Britain could have devalued or could have allowed sterling to depreciate each time sterling came under strong pressure. Depreciations might have become as frequent as they have been in Brazil, and by now the cost of living might be increasing at the rate of 100 per cent p.a. Surely it was well worth while to put up with some restrictive measures for the sake of avoiding this.

In any case, the extent of credit squeeze, wage restraint and other measures necessitated by the defence of sterling against the inflationary effects of excessive public spending, overfull employment and the misuse of the Welfare State was greatly mitigated by the substantial foreign aid obtained as a result of the Bretton Woods Agreement. Without it there would have been no big American loan in 1946, no subsequent American financial aid, no IMF drawing rights, no close Central Bank co-operation. There would be no reciprocal swap facilities, no Special Drawing Rights. It was thanks to extensive foreign assistance that the Government was able in many instances – especially since 1964 – to delay and mitigate the measures adopted when defending sterling against adverse pressure due to domestic inflation.

This aspect of the Bretton Woods system is conveniently forgotten by its critics. But those who agitate in favour of doing away with exchange stability created under the Bretton Woods system should not imagine that they could have it both ways. Since in the absence of the Bretton Woods Agreement no foreign assistance would have been forthcoming, during the late 'forties Britain would have had to choose between a runaway depreciation of the pound and much more drastic measures to defend it than those actually taken to supplement the beneficial effects of foreign financial aid. The same is true for the period since 1964. Opponents of Bretton Woods are of course not against the foreign-aid part of the system, but they would have preferred to obtain it without any 'strings' attached. Yet in the absence of restrictive measures insisted upon by creditors, Welfare State and overfull employment would have become even more inflationary and even more demoralising than they actually became during the 'sixties. Financial assistance would have been even less effective in the long run.

Even as it was, the psychological effect of the application of Welfare State and full employment in the wrong spirit produced consequences that were little short of disastrous. It was largely responsible for the series of sterling crises. The inflation it generated came frequently into conflict with Bretton Woods stability. It was not that stability, but the gross abuse of overfull employment and the Welfare State by their beneficiaries, coupled with wasteful public expenditure, that was responsible for these crises. The 'English disease' created again and again a disequilibrium between the degree of inflation in Britain and other countries. Nevertheless it was the need for maintaining sterling stable that came to be blamed for the need to adopt measures that handicapped progress.

In reality, it was mainly the increasing inadequacy of the workers' own contribution to the productive effort, and their insatiable wage demands, that were to blame for the relative slowness of Britain's growth since the war – you can't eat your cake and invest it – and for the inadequacy of the increase in the standard of living compared with that of other industrial countries.

In totalitarian States workers are forced to work by ever-present threats of drastic punitive measures, and trade unions are reduced to the subservient role of assisting the Government in the imposition of its policies on workers. In democratic countries this is, thank goodness, not possible. Nor is it possible any longer to induce workers to serve the community totally through fear of unemployment, which had provided a powerful incentive in the past. Given the Government's declared policy to avoid large-scale unemployment at all costs, and given the extent to which the Welfare State mitigates the effects of such unemployment as may occur, that incentive is no longer effective.

Some countries, such as Germany, Switzerland, the Low Countries and the Scandinavian countries, are fortunate enough to have working classes which possess a basic inclination to work. In the United States trade unions are sufficiently enlightened to realise that an increase in productivity is in the long run in accordance with the interests of their members. These countries could well afford Welfare State and full employment without having to pay the exorbitant price paid for them by Britain in the form of slower progress towards a higher standard of living.

In Britain the pursuit of unenlightened self-interest by trade unions and their members, and the absence of any genuine effort by the political parties to induce them to change their attitude, has resulted in a slow rate of growth which has prevented an increase of real wages and social service benefits at rates comparable with increases achieved in other advanced countries. All that British workers are interested in is to obtain leapfrogging unearned increases of wages even though, owing to the resulting increases in prices, much of the effect of higher wages is wiped out each time a phase of the wage–price spiral is completed.

On the face of it, unearned wage increases appear to be beneficial to the workers. They endeavour to gain unilateral advantages at the expense of their fellow workers and of other classes. They exploit their scarcity value to the utmost limit of possibility. They resent Bretton Woods stability because the restrictive measures that its maintenance forces on reluctant Governments are apt to mitigate somewhat the scarcity of labour which would enable them to plunder the community even more effectively. It is this spirit of demoralisation that is encouraged by economists agitating against the maintenance of stable exchanges.

Similar wage-induced inflation has also been proceeding in other countries, but there have been discrepancies between the respective degrees of its progress. As a result, from time to time disequilibrium developed between various currencies. In Britain such disequilibrium manifested itself in chronic balance of payments difficulties and in frequently recurring sterling crises. In the United States the disequilibrium was the result of the non-stop boom in the late 'sixties that took the place of the earlier 'stop–go–stop' policy of the 'fifties and early 'sixties. When it became inevitable for Governments to adopt disinflationary measures, the unpopularity of such measures gave rise to a growing feeling, in quite unexpected quarters, in favour of the system of floating exchanges. Politicians and businessmen alike came to assume that it would enable the United States to retain their remaining gold reserve by leaving it to private supply and demand for dollars to balance each other, instead of trying to hold the dollar at a fixed parity.

In Britain the credit squeeze in 1968–69 made floating exchanges an attractive political slogan among Conservative small businessmen who were the principal victims of credit rationing, and among debtors of all classes who had to pay interest charges at high rates that were quite unprecedented in advanced communities in modern times. It is no wonder if Mr Enoch Powell, by agitating in favour of the adoption of the floating pound, has improved his chances of capturing the leadership of the Conservative Party.

As today's troubles are always worse than yesterday's, many people are inclined to be nostalgic about the 'good old days' when in the 'thirties the Government allowed the exchanges to find their level. Even though the authorities intervened from time to time during that period to influence exchange rates, they abstained from making it a point of honour to keep sterling stable at any particular figure. The inconveniences of the flexible and floating system in the past have been forgotten, while those of the system of stable exchanges are very much in evidence in our time. For this reason politicians who favour a return to currency chaos can earn easy popularity by advocating a system that would make the world safe for unrestrained inflation. Their attitude, and the response of the public, is a flagrant manifestation of democracy at its worst.

On a number of occasions in the 'thirties Britain did in fact succeed in avoiding or mitigating the adverse effects of imported deflation by allowing sterling to depreciate. But the fact that at the outbreak of the war the unemployed were still numbered in millions must be borne in mind. To be reminded of it should serve as an antidote to the poison of presenting the period of floating exchanges as happy years.

But even if it were tempting to revert to the flexible system for the sake of avoiding a threatening excessive deflation, surely the same arguments in favour of flexibility do not apply at the time of persistently creeping and accelerating inflation and of high employment. It would be one thing to sacrifice stability to prevent the return of mass-unemployment, and quite a different thing to do so for the sake of being able to inflate for a time at an accelerated rate and with comparative impunity.

Such arguments do not seem to be able to outweigh emotional growth-hysteria which urges people to sacrifice stability for the sake of uninterrupted and ever-faster growth. There is evidence of an increasing resentment over the alleged power of the 'gnomes', under fixed exchanges, to call a halt to this growth by forcing the Government to defend sterling against the adverse pressure they create through withdrawing their balances and through speculating against sterling. It is increasingly felt that the Government had better leave foreign exchanges to find their level. It should let importers, exporters, speculators and other buyers or sellers of foreign exchanges fight each other to standstill and bring exchange rates to a level at which supply and demand balance each other.

A large number of academic economists added their weight to the demagogic campaign by politicians against stability, and their support has lent that campaign the outward appearance of respectability. Many practical men of standing – politicians, administrators, businessmen, even bankers – now are no longer afraid of finding themselves in the dubious company of radical currency cranks and politicians making a bid for popularity. So the movement against exchange stability is gathering momentum.

CHAPTER FOUR

Past Experience in Flexibility

An entire generation has grown up in Britain and in several other leading countries without any first-hand experience of the chaotic state of affairs caused by widely fluctuating exchanges during the years that followed the First World War, and again in the 'thirties. For this reason proposals for the adoption of floating exchanges, or at any rate of systems involving a more moderate degree of advanced flexibility, have come to be looked upon by many young people as bold innovations which, for that reason alone, appeal to those who fancy themselves in the role of unconventional reformers in revolt against the established order. American and British people under forty are entirely unfamiliar with the disadvantages of floating exchanges. Young theoretical and practical specialists only know about it from what they read in books. Little attention, if any, has been paid by the layman in the United States or in Britain to experience under flexibility since the war in France, in Italy and in Latin American countries.

Yet experts who favour flexibility and oppose stability cannot plead ignorance of the practical experience under the system of their preference as it actually operated in the 'fifties in Western Europe, or in countries such as Brazil right to our days. But many of the advocates of floating exchanges seem to have conveniently selective memories. When drawing on recent experience in flexible exchanges, they only seem to remember Canada, being the one instance which, given a sufficient degree of bias, can provide arguments in its favour. If they mention any other instances at all, it is only to emphasise that they occurred in 'different circumstances' which are most unlikely to recur if the flexible system were to be adopted today in their country in the particular form which they favour.

Having regard to the inadequacy of popular knowledge even about recent and present experience in flexible exchanges in general and floating exchanges in particular, and to the one-sided presentation of that experience by 'gnomocrats', a brief survey of some instances in floating and other flexible exchanges calls for no apology. In particular, as far as the younger generation is concerned it is well to remind them that, by throwing their support on the side of opponents of stability, they do not become the *avant-garde* of bold unconventional reform movements but are reactionary supporters of the return to a very ancient and discredited system from which mankind did not really emerge until the nineteenth century. Indeed the majority of countries retained their floating exchanges or other forms of flexible exchanges even in more recent times, or relapsed into them again and again. Even in our days fixed parities, maintained precariously by a relatively small number of advanced countries, are a minority, while floating exchanges or currencies subject to frequent changes of parities are the majority among less advanced countries.

When foreign exchange had assumed the form of exchanging coins, or bills of exchange payable in coins, of various countries against each other, even metallic parities, which were supposed to determine broadly the current exchange rates, were until the end of the eighteenth century flexible to an extent of being more or less floating. In the days of the Tudors more than one Royal Commission was set up with the main object of ascertaining the whereabouts of the parities known under the term 'true exchange'. The uncertainty was due to incessant changes in the relative metal contents of the various coinages, either through official action or through various forms of private debasement. So long as even *de facto* parities were floating while legal parities kept being changed by frequent recoinages or other official measures, actual exchange rates were doomed to float. Those dealing in exchanges were exposed to the uncertainties and risks that were, and still are, inherent in buying, selling, holding or owning floating currencies.

Even though the adoption of paper money constituted a step towards the modern monetary system, it had further accentuated the floating character of foreign exchanges in most countries where it came into use during the late seventeenth century and the eighteenth century. To the uncertainty of the relative metal contents of the respective coinages into which the notes were supposed to be convertible, the uncertainty of the conversion prospects of the notes into coins came to be added. The exchange rates of these notes, or of bills payable in them, fluctuated according to the assessment by the market of their chances of becoming or remaining convertible into coins. The value of the coins themselves, to be received for the notes if and when the latter should be converted, was itself highly uncertain.

Properly fixed legal parities which were also *de facto* parities did not come to be adopted until the nineteenth century, the first instance being Napoleon's franc created in 1803. Sterling continued to float until some years after the end of the Napoleonic Wars. Some other major currencies, in particular the rouble and the Austrian gulden, continued to fluctuate, or relapsed into irregular fluctuations after periods of stability, during the greater part of the nineteenth century. The U.S. dollar had its ups and downs during the early decades of the nineteenth century, and relapsed into the status of a floating currency during and for some time after the Civil War.

Exchange rates between currencies based on gold and those based on silver were floating exchange rates, fluctuating in accordance with the ever-changing gold–silver ratio, right up to the demonetisation of silver that began in the late nineteenth century and was completed between the wars. The new Latin American countries that had emerged from the Spanish and Portuguese colonial empires provided ample modern examples for floating and flexible exchanges during the nineteenth century. They were described and analysed with care by the Chilean economist Subercaseaux, whose book on the subject should be made compulsory reading for economists agitating for floating exchanges. In more recent times, too, right up to our days, several Latin American countries enjoy the doubtful blessings of floating or frequently devalued exchanges.

In all these instances, as in those of floating or frequently devalued European currencies of the inter-war period, advanced as well as backward nations had their fill of flexibility. No wonder the establishment and maintenance of stable exchanges had become the goal towards which they had striven all the time, with varying degrees of success.

Supporters of floating exchanges might resent comparisons between, say, Latin American floating exchanges during the nineteenth century or in much more recent times and the system they persistently and enthusiastically advocate for advanced industrial countries of our days. Beyond doubt, the financial, economic and political systems of some of the countries concerned had been during much of the time – and still are in some instances – in an almost perpetual disorderly state. Advocates of destabilisation could argue, at any rate to their own satisfaction, that it is quite inconceivable for leading Western European countries, the United States, Japan, etc., to get into a comparable mess in times of peace if they were to adopt floating exchanges amidst totally different conditions.

But is it really inconceivable? Is it not with the object of gaining a free hand to get precisely into such a mess for the sake of being able to offer bigger bribes to the electorates that ambitious politicians on both sides of the Atlantic want to replace Bretton Woods stability with the disorderly floating system? Are various official or unsolicited economic advisers of Governments, busily engaged in creating respectable theoretical foundations for the system of floating exchanges, aware of the responsibility they incur in making it easier for Governments to yield to temptation? Some of them at any rate, one is inclined to conclude, must surely be either knaves or fools. They are knaves if they assist in the creation of chaos through inciting politicians to destabilise, in the full knowledge of the consequences of that policy, just for the sake of achieving the adoption of their favourite inflationary schemes. They are fools if they fail to realise that the creation of chaos and of advanced inflation would be the logical, natural and inevitable outcome, in prevailing circumstances, of the adoption of the system of unrestricted fluctuations they advocate. But most of them are simply fanatical believers in the dogma of allowing market influences to take their course, and are certain that the result would necessarily benefit mankind.

Possibly many of them are affected by the prevailing growth-hysteria to such an extent that they turn a blind eye towards the excessive price their nation would have to pay for growth achieved through sacrificing stability. They choose to ignore the economic, social and political consequences of a currency chaos and of accelerating depreciation of currencies. They choose to ignore the lessons of monetary history or prefer to believe that history would not repeat itself next time if we were to revert to flexible exchanges which had produced disastrous effects in the past.

Advocates of floating exchanges may feel justified in dismissing any detailed analysis of instances of floating exchanges during earlier centuries as being 'irrelevant' – that fashionable cliché applied nowadays to almost anything one disagrees with. But the instances between the wars do deserve attention. They are conveniently set out in great factual detail by Ragnar Nurkse in *International Currency Experience*, a volume published by the League of Nations covering the inter-war period. Its chapter on 'Freely Fluctuating Exchanges' draws particular attention to some instances of the operation of pure floating exchange systems – that of the French franc from 1919 to 1926, that of sterling from the suspension of the gold standard in September 1931 until the establishment of the Exchange Equalisation Account early in 1932, and that of the dollar in 1933. In many other instances floating exchanges were subject to official intervention, but in the above instances the authorities kept aloof from the foreign exchange market.

In the case of the French franc after the First World War, the Bank of France was precluded by its statutes from selling gold at prices in excess of the official price, and under its interpretation of this rule it had to allow the franc to find its own level. So long as unreasonable hopes of an eventual return to the old parity continued to prevail, the depreciation and fluctuations of the franc were relatively moderate. By 1922, however, such hopes came to be abandoned, and four years of wide fluctuations ensued. The franc was at the mercy of speculation stimulated by inflation resulting from intractable Budgetary deficits. From time to time speculative pressures became self-aggravating, and on two major occasions, in 1924 and in 1926, they culminated in a landslide. On the first occasion it was checked and temporarily reversed with the aid of British and American bank credits. On the second occasion it was halted more effectively, thanks to the confidence inspired by Poincaré's drastic measures, leading first to the *de facto* stabilisation of the franc and two years later to its *de jure* stabilisation.

After the failure of the British authorities to save sterling in 1931 with the aid of American and French official credits, the gold standard was suspended and sterling was allowed to find its own level. The Bank of England abstained from intervening, but thanks to the drastic measures adopted by the National Government and to the nation's public-spirited response to them, the extent of sterling's depreciation remained relatively moderate. Having recovered from their reactions to the discouraging experience in intervention during the summer of 1931, the British authorities decided in 1932 to intervene systematically with the aid of the newly established Exchange Equalisation Account.

The realistic picture presented by Nurkse – a scholar of high distinction, with the wealth of factual material accumulated by the League of Nations Finance Committee at his disposal – differs fundamentally from the wishful picture presented by present-day advocates of floating exchanges. They seek to idealise the system of their choice, and to that end it suits their books to ignore the teachings of inter-war history. Those who refer to the facts of past experience at all, argue that the background against which floating exchanges would operate today is much more settled than the background against which they operated between the wars, or even during the early period after the Second World War. But a return to floating exchanges would soon re-create that selfsame background.

During the late 'forties and the 'fifties the French franc and the lira became flexible exchanges, floating from time to time freely because the authorities lacked the means or the will to intervene. They were repeatedly restabilised, devalued, allowed to find 'their own levels' again and again, with or without official intervention to influence market trends. It took the iron hands of General de Gaulle and the 'Italian miracle' to restore the stability of the two currencies. Until this was achieved, their depreciations were the cause as well as the effect of a high degree of political and economic instability.

Other former belligerent countries, too, had similar experience with floating exchanges, some of them suffering a great deal graver consequences even than France and Italy. It is difficult to find any noteworthy degree of enthusiasm for floating exchanges, or even for systems involving a less extreme degree of flexibility, in countries with recent practical experience of such systems.

The experience which advocates of floating exchange quote most frequently in support of their arguments is that of Canada. Beyond doubt, the floating Canadian dollar between 1951 and 1962 did not produce adverse effects comparable with those experienced in other countries. But the reasons why the system of flexible exchanges – it was never floating freely, for the Canadian authorities intervened systematically in the foreign exchange market – worked tolerably in Canada may be summarised as follows:

(1) Canada played the flexibility game from strength and not from weakness. The initial object of unpegging the dollar was to cope with a persistent *buying* pressure, not with a persistent *selling* pressure. It is always easier to cope with an *embarras de richesse* than with an adverse trend.

(2) Close economic and financial links between Canada and

the United States had created a permanent psychological link between the two dollars. It was widely assumed during the period of flexibility that, owing to the importance and extent of the commercial and financial connection between the two countries, the Canadian dollar would never be able to deviate too drastically from the U.S. dollar. This psychological influence greatly assisted the Canadian authorities in allowing the dollar a limited degree of freedom to fluctuate without running any real risk of a self-aggravating movement of the exchange.

(3) The flow of long-term and short-term capital between the United States and Canada has for many years been a factor of decisive influence in the market for Canadian dollars. Such movements could easily be influenced by the authorities of both countries with the aid of conventional as well as unconventional devices, in order to moderate the fluctuations of the dollar.

In spite of all the special circumstances making for a success of the system in Canada, it was indeed far from being a success. Admittedly, unlike the experiences quoted above, it was far from being a 100 per cent failure. But it did not remove the necessity for harsh monetary policy measures, nor did it save the country from a high degree of unemployment, which rose at one time to 7 per cent. Opinions in Canada are sharply divided between those who welcomed the restabilisation of the dollar and those who would have preferred to allow it to continue to fluctuate. But even experts with first-hand knowledge of the Canadian experiment who are enthusiastic supporters of flexibility candidly concede that it does not follow from Canada's experience that the same system could be operated successfully in totally different circumstances in other countries.

In any case, if the Canadian experiment had been such a success as the patron-saints of floating exchanges claim it to have been, why was it that the Canadian Government returned so soon to stability? In spite of all the mitigating circumstances which had reduced the disadvantages of floating rates to a minimum, Canada was only too glad to restabilise the dollar, expecially since during the second phase of the experiment she had to play the game from weakness and not from strength. The authorities had to intervene to keep down the extent of its depreciation.

The short-lived experiment of West Germany in floating exchanges in 1969 provided supporters of that system with another opportunity to argue that their system need not necessarily produce disastrous results. But in this instance, too, the game was played from strength – indeed from excessive strength – and not from weakness. Besides, the experiment was obviously meant to be purely temporary, pending a change of Government. More will be said about this in the concluding chapter. What is important to note is that the temporary freeing of the D. mark failed to bring the rate automatically to its equilibrium level. Its upward movement had to be assisted by official intervention to push the rate up artificially by means of heavy selling of dollars by the Bundesbank.

Experiments in floating exchanges that were played from weakness and were unaccompanied by genuine efforts to strengthen the floating currency produced unsatisfactory results. Even the British experiment of 1931 resulted in an exaggerated initial depreciation of sterling, far in excess of the extent of its overvaluation prior to the suspension of the gold standard. This might have entailed grave consequences for Britain if it had not been for the drastic deflationary measures adopted by the National Government before and immediately after the suspension of the gold standard and, above all, for the response of the British people, which willingly accepted the sacrifices imposed on it for the sake of saving the pound from extreme depreciation. But then, the main argument in favour of flexibility is precisely that the abandonment of fixed rates would make it unnecessary to impose unpopular sacrifices on the nation for the sake of defending the exchange. This argument certainly is contradicted by evidence.

Moreover the reason why the suspension of the gold standard

in 1931 assisted Britain in balancing imports by exports was that sterling became distinctly undervalued as a result of its self-aggravating downward movement. This had made British goods competitive so long as rival industrial countries maintained their old parities. But the excessive undervaluation of sterling did become the main cause of the dollar crisis that followed it. Had sterling's parities been simply adjusted to this equilibrium level by a devaluation of, say, 10 per cent in order to correct its overvaluation, instead of allowing it to depreciate by over 30 per cent for a time, the dollar crisis of 1933 with all its grave consequences might have been avoided.

As for the French experience in flexibility between the wars and in the late 'forties and 'fifties, its detailed history should be sufficient to deter anyone with an open mind from advocating the deliberate adoption of a system which was such a disastrous failure in France. It is true, the floating franc operated against a highly unfavourable background of political instability. But the frequent foreign exchange crises that resulted from the unsettling effects of the system were among the major causes of political crises as well as their effect.

CHAPTER FIVE

Why Economists Favour Floating Rates

WHY is it that the majority of theoretical economists who are now in favour of a depreciation of a currency that is under pressure, instead of a devaluation, advocate the adoption of the most extreme form of flexibility – freely floating exchange rates?

In the inter-war period the overwhelming majority of academic opinion in Britain, as in most other countries, was strictly orthodox. Most British economists endorsed the official policy of returning to the gold standard. Once Britain was back on gold, even radical economists who had opposed that change – apart from some out-and-out currency cranks such as advocates of social credit – reluctantly conceded that so long as the public preferred the gold standard to other systems it *was* the best system. Between 1925 and 1931, abandonment of stable exchanges was simply not considered to be a live issue in academic circles any more than in banking and political circles. Although the Government was frequently criticised for returning to gold, and especially for returning to the pre-1914 parity, there was no pressure on the part of any of the responsible critics in favour of a suspension of the gold standard or of devaluation of sterling. After the National Government suspended the gold standard in September 1931, a Socialist ex-Minister indignantly exclaimed: 'Nobody had told us that this could be done!' At a crisis meeting of the Economic Council, set up by Ramsay MacDonald to advise the Labour Government, which was attended by radical academic economists such as Keynes and G. D. H. Cole, no recommendation was made to that effect.

After the suspension of the gold standard – it was never

referred to as anything but a *suspension*, clearly implying that it was regarded as a temporary state of affairs – most economists took it for granted that a return to fixed gold parity was the ultimate goal, the achievement of which was a mere question of time. Disagreement on the subject was confined to the timing of restabilisation and to its circumstances.

Why is it then that the overwhelming majority of economists – even those who could not be classed as radicals in any other respect – is now against the maintenance of the relatively high degree of stability that has existed since the war? That many politicians are now against it and are agitating for floating exchanges is easily understandable. They wish to remove the need for adopting unpopular measures in defence of stable exchanges and they wish to be in a position to make and even honour election promises at the cost of inflationary overspending. No doubt some particularly politically-minded 'political' economists are inspired by similar considerations. They employ their prestige and their scholarship to create a 'respectable' theoretical background for the benefit of irresponsible politicians longing to be able to inflate with impunity.

Other economists advocate floating exchanges because, consciously or otherwise, they want to swim with the prevailing tide. They are afraid of being criticised for holding unfashionable views and of being regarded by their students as 'back numbers'. Never has there been such a strong tendency on the part of academic economists to curry favour with students, to whose opinions on foreign exchange policy they could not possibly attach much weight. No doubt they succeeded in convincing themselves by some subconscious process that, by adapting their own opinions to the latest fashions in economic thinking, they are not guilty of allowing themselves to be guided by those whom it is their duty to guide.

In the distant past academic opinion was almost without exception in favour of maintaining stability even at the cost of having to pursue deflationary policies. Yet this was at a time when deflation was the main cause of mass-unemployment and business stagnation. Economists were accused at that time of allowing themselves to be influenced by fears that to advocate a more radical policy might not be considered 'respectable'. Be that as it may, they rightly ignored suggestions made occasionally by irresponsible currency cranks that by defending the stability of currencies they were influenced, consciously or subconsciously, by their personal financial interests in defending the purchasing power of their fixed salaries.

But now, at long last, academic salaries have come to keep pace to a higher degree with the rising trend in the cost of living and with the rise in comparable professional earnings. From that point of view it is no longer essential for them to defend stability. Their change of attitude, it is now said, is in accordance with the Marxian doctrine that one's views are influenced by one's material interests. But in fairness it must be admitted that, while before the war when they stood to gain by the defence of the purchasing power of their salaries, today they would stand to gain nothing through an accentuation of inflation as a result of their volte-face. For while their emoluments might tend to keep pace with the rising trend of the cost of living that would result from the adoption of floating rates, they are not likely to be among those classes which would be in a position to enforce an increase of their income in real terms. Indeed, should the non-stop rise in prices become accentuated as a result of a heavy depreciation of the floating exchanges, there might be a time-lag before their salaries would catch up with the increase in their cost of living.

Many economists advocate floating exchanges because they have come under the influence of the prevailing growth-hysteria. Expansion at all costs and to the full limit of economic and technological possibilities is the fashionable objective. Of course everybody, with the exception of puritans who disapprove of increasing prosperity – because they believe that we must have a thoroughly miserable time in this world in order to deserve to have a good time in the next – is in favour of economic growth. But some of us still believe what was generally regarded as axiomatic by economists before the war – that, even from the point of view of achieving the maximum of growth in the long run, it pays to interrupt expansion from time to time for the sake of consolidating progress achieved. Taking a long view, such interruptions, and even moderate setbacks, save us from major setbacks inflicted on the community sooner or later by unduly sharp or unduly prolonged uninterrupted expansion.

Before the war it was all but generally realised, at any rate in academic circles, that prolonged booms entailed the risk of slumps and prolonged depressions. But because the world has now had some decades without a major slump, it has come to be taken widely for granted that such slumps are a matter of the past and that, thanks to our higher skill in managing economic trends, booms could now go on for ever.

Yet economists ought to know that human nature has not changed. In the prolonged absence of minor setbacks, producers and merchants gradually drift into unsound practices. They feel safe in assuming that the favourable conditions making for ever-increasing profits and capital gains would continue for ever. Unsound positions are liable to develop in such conditions: too much indiscriminate expansion of producing capacity, unselective increase of output and inventories, overtrading, overlending and overborrowing. Above all, there is overconsumption in both the private and public sectors of the economy. Consumers mortgage their incomes too far ahead on the assumption that those incomes are safe and their increase is certain. They incur too heavy commitments. Governments and local authorities become overambitious and increasingly wasteful in their expenditure. Producers, merchants and consumers become too vulnerable. Investors, too, come to assume that they have concluded a contract with providence for the continuation of an everlasting rise of Stock Exchange prices, even though the current prices have discounted all future expansion that could be reasonably expected for a long series of years. They spend their capital gains and make no provision for capital losses. Unsound and vulnerable positions tend to arise in every direction.

Production under non-stop booms is apt to become wasteful,

albeit in a different sense from that prevailing under large-scale unemployment. Since even inefficient producers could depend to a reasonable degree on making tolerable profits amidst creeping inflation, there is less incentive for managements to become more efficient. They can afford to 'hoard' redundant labour for future requirements and to submit without resistance to trade union restrictive practices.

As for labour, owing to the change in the balance of power in favour of trade unions resulting from the non-stop boom, it is bound to become less efficient and more costly. Higher and higher wages are enforced in return for less and less work. There are frequent strikes, both official and unofficial, and other forms of industrial action or inaction. The pressure of consumer demand resulting from inflationary increases in wages unaccompanied by correspondingly higher productivity lulls producers and merchants into a false feeling of optimism.

The boom in equities creates capital gains that stimulate luxury trades to satisfy ever-increasing luxury spendings which are no longer confined to upper income groups. Such trades could not be expected to survive once the trend is reversed. Hire-purchase liabilities, which tend to become dangerously high, become a major source of potential crises.

Britain has been affected by wage inflation even under fixed parities to a higher degree than most other advanced industrial countries, largely owing to the inadequate increase in her output caused by inadequate investment and industrial indiscipline. Hence the frequently recurrent sterling crises. It is certain that the 'English disease' would become greatly aggravated under flexible exchanges. There would be much less inducement to put on the brake on unearned wage increases from time to time and to restrain the obscene plundering of the community by trade unions.

Since various countries would not inflate to the same extent under floating exchanges, discrepancies would increase between their respective rates of inflation. They would frequently create disequilibrium, far in excess of those under fixed parities. This would give rise to balance of payments problems. The resulting foreign exchange problems would of course be allowed to solve themselves by depreciation and still more depreciation of the weak exchanges.

It would be a matter of common sense to interrupt non-stop booms and creeping inflation from time to time, not only for the sake of defending the exchange value of the national currency, but also for the sake of defending its domestic purchasing power and for the sake of consolidating from time to time the progress achieved. *Reculer pour mieux sauter* may be a cliché, but it contains profound wisdom all the same. When under fixed parities the brake has to be applied to defend the exchange, as often as not the right thing happens for the wrong reasons. After an interruption, expansion can be resumed more safely.

During the 'fifties and the early and middle 'sixties most advanced countries pursued a policy of 'stop–go–stop' under which expansion was consolidated from time to time. Deliberate policies of managing the economy were necessary in order to ensure a reasonable degree of stability in the long run. Such policies came to be adopted not for the sake of maintaining a balanced domestic economy, but to avoid external instability assuming the form of foreign exchange crises and dangerous declines of reserves. The basic cause of such crises was of course inadequate domestic stability. But had it not been for the effect of domestic instability on exchanges and reserves, it is safe to assume that most Governments would have done little or nothing to restore equilibrium.

Needless to say, measures to restore equilibrium are always very unpopular, especially in Britain and in the United States, as these countries have caught the disease of growth-hysteria. Germany, Italy, Japan, France until recently, and some of the smaller continental industrial countries have been much more willing to put up with 'stop–go–stop' in order to avoid the alternative – 'boom–slump'. Britain and in recent years also the United States, on their part, preferred to expand unhindered. They have come to expect the more conservative nations to finance their resulting balance of payments deficit in some form or other – Britain through borrowing, the United

States through inducing surplus countries to retain their surpluses in the form of dollars. It is in these countries that the system of floating exchanges finds the strongest academic and political support, because of the fear that sooner or later even the most ingenious and sophisticated methods of financing their deficits might exhaust the limits of their possibilities to borrow. British and American opinion has become increasingly favourable towards adopting a formula under which they would not have to call a halt to expansion because of mere balance of payments deficits. They would prefer to pay the cost of inflation in the form of exchange instability instead of continuing to pay it in the form of declining reserves and increasing external indebtedness.

A basic reason for the preference of so many economists for floating exchanges is that they think only in terms of abstract theory instead of thinking also in terms of practical realities. One of the leading exponents of the theory of floating exchanges, Professor Egon Sohmen, candidly admits that he is 'inclined to be considerably more cautious in advocating flexible rates as a feasible policy' than he is in outlining their superiority on purely logical grounds. In other words, advocacy of the system of floating rates may be justified as an intellectual parlour-game, but even some of its supporters have doubts as to whether it is a suitable basis for practical policy decisions that affect the lives of every man, woman and child.

Professor Sohmen is aware that Governments might possibly abuse their freedom gained through the removal of the discipline imposed on them by fixed parities. He is also aware of the need for reducing the monopolistic power of trade unions and of business interests in order to be safe to adopt floating rates without risking a flight of capital, a snowballing of crises, fall of exchanges and a rise in prices. Understandably enough, he envisages the possibility that the system of floating exchanges might become discredited if it should produce such results. As a determined supporter of that system, however, he appears to have found no difficulty in reassuring himself, after some hesitation, that politicians, trade unionists and monopolistic business firms would all play the game according to the rules once the system of his choice has come to be adopted. Yet it is difficult to find a valid reason for the optimistic assumption that these sectional interests would cease to be selfish under the system of floating exchanges, even though that system would greatly encourage their selfishness.

Many economists are in favour of floating exchanges because of their belief in economic and monetary internationalism. They believe that the defence of stable exchanges at a fixed rate might lead to economic nationalism in the form of exchange controls and foreign trade controls adopted for the sake of defending the exchanges at their minimum support points. They take it for granted, therefore, that the adoption of floating rates would obviate the necessity for such controls and that under that system even the remaining controls could be removed. Free fluctuations of exchange rates would, according to them, give rise to more freedom of international movements of goods and capital. This hope is based on the assumption that Governments would share their implicit faith that correct exchange rates would emerge from the free fluctuations of exchanges. With a remarkable unscholarly piece of question-begging, they assume that whatever exchange rate emerges from free fluctuations in the complete absence of any form of Government interference would be the right rate.

But politicians and administrators could not afford to be quite so dogmatic. It seems probable that in a wide variety of situations the authorities would have distinct preferences for exchange rates that would differ materially from the rates emerging through free fluctuations. They might try to influence the rates by means of conventional monetary policy – which would mean in practice a return to stop–go – or by intervention in the foreign exchange market with the aid of accumulated or borrowed foreign exchange reserves. But they might find all this insufficient to enforce their policy, in which case they might be strongly tempted to revert to controls. Indeed the chances are that, when movements of freely fluctuating exchanges become self-aggravating, the imperative need for restraining their exaggerated trends might necessitate even more drastic Government intervention in various forms than does the defence of fixed rates. Runaway depreciation of an exchange might frighten the Government into extreme panic measures to check it at all costs.

Amidst waves of frantic speculation, the temptation to restore stability by adopting drastic controls would be very high. In fact, both between the wars and since the war countries with freely depreciating currencies did resort on many occasions to various forms of advanced exchange control. There were moreover many instances of protectionist measures to safeguard local industries from exchange dumping on the part of countries with depreciating and undervalued currencies.

But even if it were correct to assume that floating rates would obviate the necessity for exchange and trade controls, it would not mean that the system would be nearer to the ideal international economy of theoretical economists than the system of stable currencies. For the object of adopting floating exchanges is precisely to isolate the economy of the country that adopts the system from the economies of other countries. The reason why supporters of the system agitate for the abandonment of fixed parities is precisely to be able to pursue monetary, financial, economic, social, technological and military policies independently of international monetary influences. If in pursuing costly policies the country's economy gets out of equilibrium in relation to other countries, its floating exchange rates would be expected to offset the resulting gap in its balance of payments that would arise in such circumstances under fixed parities. Governments hope to be able to pursue policies regardless of their material and psychological effects on their exchanges.

It would be difficult to justify the contention that such a change would make for a more integrated international economy. Indeed the logical outcome of floating rates would be competitive depreciation races similar to those experienced in the 'thirties – a form of financial and economic warfare in time of peace.

Another possible explanation of the popularity of floating rates among academic economists is their deeply-rooted attachment to *laisser-faire*. This sentiment has gained in strength since the war, as a reaction to the increase of Government intervention in many economic spheres, and particularly in the sphere of foreign exchange. Hence the feeling that the Government should keep out of foreign exchange altogether. Not only should there be no exchange control, but it should not be the Government's task to determine or influence the exchange value of the national currency. Indeed, some advocates of floating rates go so far as to argue that Governments should abstain even from allowing their conventional monetary policy measures to be guided by any desire to influence the trend of the exchanges. Let the exchanges simply take care of themselves.

In practice, if self-aggravating exchange movements should develop, the Government might drift into intervention, not to keep the rate fixed but to prevent or moderate unwanted or exaggerated movements. As in a great many instances in the 'thirties, in practice it would be Governments that would determine changes in exchange rates. Surely that would be a very high form of active Government interference with the economy, a much higher degree of interference than the passive policy involved in pegging the rates. Moreover, since a deliberate depreciation of the exchange – or even a policy of allowing it to depreciate unhindered – constitutes a bounty to exports and protection against imports, the policy of causing or allowing the exchange deliberately to depreciate is indeed very far removed from *laisser-faire*. It is a form of aggressive economic nationalism, a revival of the 'beggar-my-neighbour' policy pursued in the 'thirties.

Of course, even co-ordinated adjustments of fixed parities, or changes in parities such as the British devaluation of 1967 or the French devaluation of 1969, are liable to be detrimental to the interests of other countries. But both devaluations aimed at reducing to a minimum the harm caused to other countries. Admittedly the borderline between adjustment correcting unfair disadvantages and adjustments securing unfair advantages is very indistinct and uncertain. But surely it is a more civilised principle to aim, or even to pretend to aim, at making a fair adjustment than to pursue a ruthless policy of currency depreciation races which would almost inevitably mean in practice excessive depreciations giving rise to similarly excessive depreciations of other exchanges as a result of allowing unregulated fluctuations of floating exchanges to take their course, or of deliberately exaggerating their movement.

Throughout this chapter, as indeed throughout the book, we have been mainly concerned with the effects of a depreciation of a floating exchange on an adverse balance. There have been only casual references to the impact of an appreciation on an export surplus. But arguments employed in connection with depreciation apply also to movements in the opposite sense. Influences similar to those which prevent the elimination of a deficit by allowing the exchange to depreciate to a theoretical equilibrium rate also operate in an opposite sense. Appreciation as well as depreciation are liable to be self-aggravating.

The only basic difference – one of major importance – is that while prices and wages are flexible and respond to depreciation, they are much less flexible when it comes to responding to appreciation. Government intervention to prevent an unwanted appreciation – a flagrant departure from *laisser-faire* in the view of purist advocates of floating exchanges – would be much more effective than departure from neutrality in the opposite sense. What matters from the point of view of the argument with which we are here concerned is that adoption of floating exchanges for the sake of the pursuit of *laisser-faire* is apt to become self-defeating.

Politicians and pseudo-economists have invented a particularly clever piece of sophistry in support of this policy. They argue that, just as it is wrong for Governments to encroach upon the sphere of the private sector of the economy by fixing the prices of goods and services, it is equally wrong to fix the value of money. This argument is likely to make many converts among those who disapprove of price controls. But the comparison suggested by the argument is absolutely fallacious.

There are certain spheres in which it is the Government's supreme duty to intervene, and the determination of the value of money is one of them. Those who argue against it on the ground that it means encroachment into the sphere of market economy would also have to demand, in order to be consistent, the repeal of the Companies Acts and all other legislation adopted to safeguard legitimate private and public interests. Why make it compulsory for limited liability companies to observe any rules imposed on them by legislation? Let their shareholders safeguard their interests in the best way they can, unaided by the Government or by law courts.

Why not repeal all traffic regulations in the sacred name of freedom? Let motorists drive on any side of the streets, at any speed, and let them park anywhere. The result would be utter chaos. But then the same result would be produced in the economic sphere if the Government relinquished its responsibility for the determination of the value of money. The difference is that chaotic traffic conditions could be brought under control very easily, while it would be extremely difficult to emerge from the chaos created by uncontrolled exchanges. And the cost of the experiment would be extremely high.

This is what economists agitating for floating rates refuse to realise. They firmly believe that pure *laisser-faire* has only advantages in all circumstances and no conceivable disadvantages. They accept uncritically the myth that freely fluctuating exchange rates are bound to gravitate towards their trade equilibrium level at which imports and exports would balance. This fallacy will be dealt with in the next chapter.

CHAPTER SIX

The Equilibrium Rate Myth

THE theoretical case in favour of floating rates, while influenced by the various considerations dealt with in the last chapter, is based overwhelmingly on the belief, held firmly by virtually all academic economists, in the existence of an ideal rate at which imports and exports would automatically balance. According to this belief, all that is needed is to allow the exchange rate to float to that rate, and troublesome import surpluses or export surpluses would disappear. A floating exchange would then tend to remain around this equilibrium rate and this would keep imports and exports permanently balanced.

Never in the history of economic thought and policy has such an utterly fallacious view been held by so many with such fanatical conviction.

Of course none of those who believe in this equilibrium rate myth pretend to be able to calculate or even estimate that ideal rate. They do not even attempt to provide an adequate formula on which their theory is based. In a different sphere, Professor Cassel made some such attempt half a century ago by producing his Purchasing Power Parity Theory, according to which exchange rates are determined by relative price levels. In spite of its many defects, that theory is a much more intelligent presentation of the argument trying to prove the existence of an equilibrium rate for exchanges than any of the theories put forward in recent years to prove the existence of an equilibrium rate for foreign trade. But Cassel's formula is out of fashion – when I was addressing the Marshall Society some years ago I found that otherwise highly intelligent members of my audience had never even heard of it – and no similar static theory that is nearly as adequate has taken its place. It seems that the existence of a trade equilibrium level of exchange rates is simply considered axiomatic, and that it is deemed to be the worst of heresies to doubt that dogma.

Exchange rates are supposed to adapt themselves to their trade equilibrium level and, minor fluctuations apart, to settle down around it in the absence of Government interference preventing this either by intervention in the foreign exchange market or by fixing artificial parities and defending them by various monetary, economic and fiscal measures.

It is understandable that advocates of floating exchanges should believe in such an equilibrium rate. After all, their faith in it constitutes the very basis of their belief in the miraculous effects of floating rates. What is much more difficult to understand is that even some opponents of floating exchanges deem it necessary to pay lip-service to this creed, presumably because to profess belief in the existence of a trade equilibrium rate is a form of intellectual or pseudo-intellectual snobbery. Theoretical economists, even if they are against floating exchanges, feel they owe it to their academic status to profess to believe in it. They have not the moral courage to repudiate it. Yet the supposed existence of such an equilibrium rate is by far the strongest theoretical argument in favour of floating rates. If the assumption of its existence is accepted, the whole theoretical case against floating rates collapses. To be consistent, economists who believe in the equilibrium rate myth ought to believe in the theoretical justification of letting exchanges take care of themselves.

Let me give a flagrant instance of the unintelligent inconsistency of which those who believe in the equilibrium rate myth but reject floating exchanges on theoretical grounds are guilty. In my book *Foreign Exchange Crises* I criticised economists who believed in the existence of a trade equilibrium level. Reviewing my book in the *Journal of Economic Literature*, Professor P. M. Kenen reacted to my criticism in the following terms: 'Many economists, including this reviewer, have doubts about the case for full flexibility. . . . But *we can do without this sort of assistance*' (my italics). If even opponents of floating rates treat disbelief in the dogmatic foundations of that policy with contempt, can supporters of the system be blamed for turning a blind eye towards the obvious fallacy of their theoretical argument?

As we propose to show in Chapter 13, the case for floating exchanges can be discredited independently of theoretical considerations, on the practical ground that under that system the volume of forward exchange facilities available for trade would be liable to become deficient. But very few theoretical economists are sufficiently familiar with the technique of the foreign exchange market to realise and appreciate this practical aspect of the subject. The controversy is waged on purely theoretical grounds, and opponents of floating exchanges who concede to their antagonists that the latter's basic argument is correct are like generals who order their army to discard their most effective weapons in the middle of the battle.

It is my contention that the case for floating exchanges rests on a false theory which grossly oversimplifies an extremely complicated situation for the sake of producing a neat model calculated to impress their fellow members of the mutual admiration society that is more concerned with the 'elegant' formal presentation of a theory than with the realities it is supposed to express. If these model-builders merely played an intellectual or pseudo-intellectual parlour-game, little harm would be done. But those who play it would assume grave responsibility if they succeeded in overpersuading responsible statesmen to stake the welfare of their countries on the belief in the myth on which the theory is based.

My attack on the overwhelming majority of economists, many of whom are of first-rate standing and command high respect in the sphere of economic theory, would be doomed to failure if I were not in a position to defy their combined weight of authority, and expose the fallacy they endorse, by substantiating my charges. This is what I shall try to do in this chapter and in the next four chapters.

The substance of my contention is that there are other equilibrium levels for foreign exchanges, besides their trade equilibrium level, at which imports and exports should balance. And since an exchange rate can only conform to one equilibrium level at a time, then, as a matter of simple arithmetic, if it is at its trade equilibrium level it is bound to be out of equilibrium in relation to the other equilibrium levels. There must necessarily exist a tendency for the rate to adapt itself to some extent to the other equilibrium levels as well, by deviating from its trade equilibrium level. The tendency in the foreign exchange market is towards an *overall* equilibrium between aggregate supply and aggregate demand, irrespective of whether the supply and demand originated through trade or capital movements or speculation or arbitrage. The market trend of exchange rates is determined by the combined effect of transactions arising from all sources. Unless by some remote chance all equilibrium levels happen to be identical, the rate at which total supply and total demand fight each other to standstill is bound to differ from the rate at which supply and demand originating from foreign trade alone fight each other to standstill.

It is understandable if theoretical economists, being unfamiliar with foreign exchange practice, are unaware of the existence of technical limitations to the volume of forward exchange facilities under floating exchanges and of my argument in Chapter 13 based on those limitations. There can be, however, no excuse or even extenuating circumstances for them to overlook the elementary theoretical argument based on the plurality of equilibrium levels and the impossibility of an exchange rate adapting itself to more than one of the levels at any given moment. Nor can they conceivably believe that the influence of the trade equilibrium level on the exchange rate is so overwhelmingly important all the time that the influence of the other equilibrium levels must be a negligible quantity. From time to time, dealings on commercial account are overshadowed by dealings on capital account or on speculative account, or even on arbitrage account. On such occasions the rate is bound to diverge considerably from its trade equilibrium level, and the rate that emerges from the combined effect of all equilibrium levels does not ensure equilibrium between imports and exports.

There can be only two conceivable situations in which a freely floating exchange rate gravitates without hindrance towards its trade equilibrium level and tends to remain around that level:

(1) If the equilibrium levels for capital movements, speculation and arbitrage happen to be identical with the equilibrium level for trade.

(2) If tendencies making for the deviation of the exchange rate from its trade equilibrium level, caused by discrepancies between the various non-commercial equilibrium levels, cancel each other out, so that the non-commercial influences in the foreign exchange market are on balance 'neutral'.

Either of these situations may be theoretically conceivable, but in practice they are utterly unlikely to arise, except through a remarkable degree of coincidence bordering on miracle which could exist for brief periods only. As we shall see in the next four chapters, the equilibrium rates for capital movements, for speculation, and for arbitrage are affected by sets of influence that are largely different from those affecting foreign trade. There is admittedly a tendency for the effect of speculation on the exchange rate to be cancelled out by covered interest arbitrage operations. But there is no similar built-in tendency for the combined effects of speculation, arbitrage and capital movements to fight each other to standstill, leaving the field clear for commercial transaction to determine exchange rates in such a way as to ensure equilibrium between imports and exports.

As the foreign exchange market is a good market, excess supply or excess demand always finds a counterpart, so that aggregate supply always equals aggregate demand even during periods when there is a wide gap between supply and demand on purely commercial account. In the absence of non-commercial transactions, commercial supply and commercial demand could only balance through a reduction of imports and/or an increase of exports until the amount of transactions arising from the two meet. But since there are always non-commercial transactions, total supply and total demand in foreign exchanges can, and does, offset each other even if there is an import surplus or an export surplus.

Moreover each one of the non-commercial sources of foreign exchange transactions is much more elastic than commercial transactions. Capital transfers, speculative transactions or arbitrage transactions can be arranged and executed in a matter of minutes, while it may take days, weeks and months before imports and exports can be arranged and before foreign exchange transactions arising from them reach the market. This means that it is incomparably easier and quicker for non-commercial transactions than for commercial transactions to fill gaps between the supply and demand of foreign exchanges caused by import or export surpluses long before foreign exchange transactions reaching the market through imports are reduced, and/or those reaching the market through exports are increased, sufficiently to meet an excess of demand for exchanges over supply. The gap is filled by non-commercial transactions.

It is a theoretical absurdity and a practical impossibility to expect an exchange rate to settle at a level at which imports and exports balance. The chances that capital transactions, speculative transactions and arbitrage transactions might happen to balance at the same figure as commercial transactions are so remote as to be virtually non-existent. If only one of these three categories of transactions is out of balance at the trade equilibrium rate, the exchange rate cannot settle at a figure at which transactions arising from imports and exports balance.

Admittedly, the state of the balance on commercial account, and its changes resulting from exchange movements, influences capital movements, speculation and arbitrage. But it is far from being the only factor influencing them. We shall see in Chapters 8, 9 and 10 that capital movements, speculative operations and arbitrage transactions are influenced by sets of factors independent of changes in supply–demand relationship on commercial account, and largely independent of exchange movements resulting from those changes.

The whereabouts of the four principal equilibrium rates are affected by four distinct sets of factors. Some of these factors overlap, but most of them either don't react to each other or only react to each other indirectly or inadequately. There is no automatic trend to bring them together. Deviations of exchange rates from any of the equilibrium levels tend to lead to excess of a total demand over supply, and equilibrium is restored at a rate which does not correspond to either of the four equilibrium levels.

Even the equilibrium rate for trade alone is no simple matter, especially if we bear in mind that invisible items also have to be taken into consideration. But let us imagine, for the sake of argument, that there is an exchange rate at which a trade deficit is eliminated because it is low enough to make locally produced goods cheap for foreigners and to make foreign goods dear for local buyers, so that between them the reduction in the value of imports and the increase in value of exports establishes balance on trade account. We propose to show in the next chapter how utterly unlikely it is – even in the complete absence of interference with the process by non-commercial influences affecting aggregate supply and demand in the foreign exchange market – that such a rate should ever remain in force for more than a short time.

If we envisage a fairly wide range of rates – trade equilibrium *level* instead of trade equilibrium *rate* – it is just conceivable that the period of equilibrium might continue for a short time, provided that the spread is wide enough to cover widely different rates. But it would be quite a different range from the one within which speculative supply and demand, *and* supply and demand arising from arbitrage, *and* supply and demand arising from capital movements, would balance each other.

It is essential to realise a fact which, elementary as it is, appears to be ignored by advocates of floating exchanges – that supply and demand in the foreign exchange market always balance because a counterpart to excess supply or excess demand is always forthcoming at a price. In a disorderly market there may be some slight delay in the adjustment of the rates to a figure at which they attract the necessary counterpart, but even if at a given moment buying orders or selling orders predominate and counterparts are reluctant in forthcoming, it is because the would-be buyers or the would-be sellers are unwilling to pay or accept the rates at which counterparts would become readily available. If they are keen enough to buy or sell, the balance between supply and demand is soon restored.

If we disregard such frictional delays, the foreign exchange market is like a balance sheet – its two sides are always bound to balance. To carry the comparison further, if a balance sheet is only 'balanced' by the item represented by the amount of the unpaid liabilities which the firm is unable to pay or which its insolvent debtors are unable to pay, the balancing of the credit side and the debit side does not mean in any sense that all is well with the firm concerned. Likewise, if supply and demand on the foreign exchange market are only balanced through increases in short positions or long positions induced by a change in the exchange rates, it does not mean in any sense that the economy of the country concerned, as indicated by its exchange, is at equilibrium. There is certainly no need for imports and exports to balance in order to ensure equilibrium in the foreign exchange market. Equilibrium between supply and demand in that market is virtually continuous irrespective of the ups and downs of the gap between supply and demand on commercial account alone. There is no need for the exchange rate to adapt itself to a level at which imports and exports balance to ensure overall equilibrium at which the exchange rate may remain stable for the duration of that equilibrium.

As in respect of balance sheets so in respect of the foreign exchange market, what matters is the way in which the two sides are balanced. If a trade deficit is balanced through an increase in the deficit country's foreign short-term indebtedness, it is far from being a satisfactory state of affairs. Even if a current trade deficit is balanced through a surplus of long-term capital imports, it is not necessarily a satisfactory state of affairs. But the result of capital imports can be a state of equilibrium in the market in spite of a perennial trade deficit. Conversely, overlending abroad or other forms of capital export – such as a flight of national capital – may cause an adverse pressure on a currency in spite of its export surplus. This was the case with the lira in 1969.

A depreciation of an exchange caused by an import surplus need not restore the balance between supply and demand on commercial account, even if it does increase exports and reduces imports. It might cause adverse capital movements such as withdrawals of foreign funds or a flight of national capital, which would more than offset the effect of the depreciation on imports and exports. We shall see in Chapter 8 that both short-term and long-term capital movements are largely independent of the foreign trade position and also of exchange movements, and need not balance an import surplus or an export surplus. They might even prevent imports and exports from balancing, or they might unbalance them, through influencing exchange rates and making them deviate from the level at which imports and exports would balance.

The existence of four different equilibrating or disequilibrating sets of influences, and the fact that they are independent from each other to a very large extent, rules out for all practical purposes the possibility of exchange rates being determined solely by their trade equilibrium level at which imports and exports would balance. The actual exchange rate that emerges through the combined effect of the four different sets of influences is bound to differ from each of the four individual equilibrium levels.

Hitherto we have been dealing only with spot rates. The discrepancies between spot and forward rates introduce another element of complication which further removes the likelihood of achieving balanced foreign trade through allowing spot rates to float freely. Even if the spot rate were to attain and settle around its theoretical trade equilibrium level, it would not necessarily mean that imports and exports would balance in practice. For forward rates might deviate from that level for a variety of reasons. In normal conditions forward margins are largely determined by interest parities – the differential between the level of interest rates in the two countries concerned. For a detailed discussion of this technical point the reader must be referred to my *Dynamic Theory of Forward Exchange*. Even under perfectly normal conditions forward rates are liable to differ materially from spot rates owing to the existence of interest differentials. The difference might be reduced or exaggerated by speculation, hedging, leads and lags, capital movements and arbitrage.

As a high proportion of foreign trade is transacted with the aid of forward exchange transactions, the equilibrium level of spot exchange rates at which imports and exports would balance if all trade were financed with spot exchange is affected by the premium or discount on forward exchanges. If the forward rate of a country with an import surplus is at a heavy discount, a smaller degree of depreciation of the spot rate is sufficient to eliminate the import surplus – provided that the depreciation of the spot rate is not accompanied by a narrowing of the discount on the forward rate. In reality the chances are that a depreciation of the spot rate which is floating towards its trade equilibrium level tends to widen the discount in anticipation of a further depreciation until the spot rate comes to command confidence in the market. This may mean that imports and exports may tend to balance before the spot rate has completed its depreciation to its theoretical trade equilibrium level, because a large part of the foreign trade is financed with depreciated forward exchange. In practice the trade equilibrium level must be some combination of the levels of spot and forward rates. For this reason equilibrium is liable to be upset by changes in the forward margin, by the proportion of foreign trade that is financed by means of forward exchange transactions, and by changes in the average length of such forward exchange transactions. To disregard this influence oversimplifies the theory of floating exchanges.

CHAPTER SEVEN

The Trade Equilibrium Level

THE idea that an intractable balance of payments deficit could be eliminated with the proverbial stroke of the pen, by simply removing fixed parities and allowing the exchange rate to depreciate to a level at which imports are balanced by exports, could be described as touchingly naïve if its presentation were not so elaborate and oversophisticated. Here we were, struggling hard to export more and import less, submitting to credit squeeze, wage freeze and other unpleasant devices, when all that the Government would have had to do was to follow the advice thrust upon it by a multitude of economists to let sterling find its own level. Our trade would then have balanced and it would not have been necessary to inflict hardships on us.

How simple it all sounds. It is a thousand pities that it is all wrong. Life would be ever so much less unpleasant to the Government and to the governed alike if the Government could cheerfully divest itself of the responsibility for taking difficult decisions and for resorting to unpleasant measures in the interests of balancing imports and exports. Let the foreign exchange market and all the multitude of firms and individuals who deal in exchanges directly or indirectly do the deciding for the Government and for the nation.

But let us remember that even if the market could solve our problem of balancing foreign trade, it would still be necessary for the Government to decide whether the disadvantages arising from the degree of depreciation required for balancing foreign trade would not be an excessive price to pay for the achievement of equilibrium. The possibility that the equilibrium, even if restored at the cost of a heavy depreciation of the exchange, might well prove to be purely temporary must also be taken into consideration. For it is one thing to submit to a depreciation of, say, 25 per cent for the sake of solving our balance of payments problem once for all, and quite another to submit to it for the sake of achieving balance for five minutes.

In any case, however, it would be ever so nice to know for certain that we could solve, if we wanted to, even the most intractable balance of payments problem by taking the line of least resistance. It would be satisfactory to feel that there is no need for hard work or self-restraint for the sake of avoiding inflation, since now that we have become enlightened at long last about the way in which to handle the effects of inflation on the balance of payments we shall be free to inflate with impunity.

Of course we have no means of knowing the whereabouts of the exchange rate at which imports and exports are supposed to balance. Fortunately there is, according to advocates of floating exchanges, no need for us to know it. If only we would let sterling float freely it would float automatically to the right level. All we have to do is to let it float without hindrance.

Some would-be miracle-mongers carry even further their childlike faith in the all-curing effect of the simple expedient of letting the exchange float to the level at which our problem would solve itself. They expect the device to solve not only our balance of payments problem but also our employment problem. According to them, the exchange should be allowed to depreciate to a level at which imports and exports would balance *at full employment*. This assumes that a depreciation of the exchange would increase employment, through reducing imports and increasing exports, until a stage is reached at which the trade deficit is eliminated at precisely the same time when unemployment ceases. They fail to explain why and how the two events should become automatically synchronised, but the theory seems to suggest by implication that trade deficit is the sole cause of unemployment, so that when the former disappears the latter also disappears.

It is true that in given circumstances an improvement of the trade balance results in a reduction of unemployment. But Britain's experience in 1964–66 shows that an increasing degree of overfull employment can coexist with a perennial trade deficit. And it is all but generally admitted that an increase in unemployment, by reducing domestic demand, tends to improve the balance of payments.

Of course those who believe in the possibility of making the disappearance of the trade deficit coincide with the disappearance of unemployment think in terms of inter-war economic conditions, when there was ample unused industrial capacity that could be reduced through 'exporting unemployment' by means of exchange dumping with the aid of an undervalued currency, and through protection against imports provided by the undervalued currency. But in the conditions of practically full employment prevailing in Britain and in some other industrial countries today, the theory would be simply irrelevant even if it were not in in any case inherently false. An export boom superimposed on a fully employed currency would only mean more wage inflation, not more employment.

It seems by no means certain whether currency depreciation is necessarily able to eliminate either balance of payments deficit or unemployment even if there is unused producing capacity. For one thing, when assessing the advantages of the system of floating exchanges its advocates usually envisage its adoption by one single country. They assume that the other countries would meekly submit to economic aggression in the form of exchange dumping and of additional trade barriers against imports through an undervaluation of the currency. They assume that the victims of economic aggression would simply allow the economic aggressor to gain and retain all the fruits of his aggression, without taking any defensive or retaliatory action to safeguard their vital and legitimate interests. Yet, judging by past experience, Governments confronted with exchange dumping and import reduction through a depreciation of the exchanges of rival countries are in the habit of assuming the role of the proverbial wicked animal – *cet animal est méchant, quand on l'attaque il se défend.* They would defend their economies by export subsidies and protective trade measures and/or by competitive currency depreciation. In any case the pressure that causes a currency to depreciate is liable to be shifted on other currencies once the currency that started the depreciation race ceased to be overvalued. There would be a series of leapfrogging depreciations in the course of which each currency in turn would become undervalued and overvalued.

The extent to which currency depreciations are capable of improving the balance of payments as well as the extent to which they can increase employment is very far from being a matter of simple arithmetic. It is a matter of sheer guesswork. Judging by the experience of the British devaluation of 1967 and the French devaluation of 1969, it need not necessarily be the case, at any rate not for some time. If our unused producing capacity is limited – as it was in Britain at the time of the devaluation of 1967 – exports cannot be increased without also increasing imports to a more or less corresponding extent, unless and until the output is increased through harder or more efficient work. For, given the extent of domestic consumer demand, any diversion of goods from the home market to exports would automatically increase imports which are needed to satisfy home demand that is left unsatisfied as a result of the reduction of supplies in consequence of increased exports.

But even if we accepted for the sake of argument that the output could be increased simultaneously with a depreciation of the floating sterling, there is no reason whatsoever for assuming that an exchange rate which ensures sufficient exchange dumping would ensure sufficient protection to increase production until full employment is achieved. The rates of exchange at which exchange depreciation might achieve the two objectives – balancing foreign trade and achieving full employment – would be in all probability quite different. For this reason alone the additional complication introduced into the theory of floating exchanges by claiming that the two objectives could be attained at the same exchange rate should be dismissed as entirely absurd. Serious argument should be confined to the balance of payments aspect of currency depreciation.

Even in such a less ambitious form, the theory is utterly divorced from reality. It would only be valid in the following circumstances:

(1) If no country took retaliatory or defensive action.
(2) If no other country allowed its exchange to float.
(3) If elasticity of supply, demand and prices were high.
(4) If the depreciation did not affect leads and lags on imports and exports.
(5) If it did not affect capital movements, speculation or arbitrage.
(6) If exchange rates were not affected by capital movements, speculation or arbitrage.

Subject to such conditions it would be theoretically conceivable that the effect of exchange depreciation on the value of imports and exports would be sufficient, in addition to offsetting its effect on the terms of trade – changes in which could not be excluded even for the sake of abstract argument – to wipe out the deficit by increasing the volume of exports and reducing the volume of imports to the required extent.

But in practice there is also the snag of the inevitable time-lag between changes in exchange rates and their effects on imports and exports. For well over twelve months after the devaluation of sterling in 1967 we still kept hearing that its effects on exports were yet to come. As far as capital equipment is concerned the time-lag might well be twelve months or more. Had sterling been unpegged in 1967 instead of being devalued during the interval, it would have depreciated well beyond its trade equilibrium level. If, instead of being held firmly at above $2.38 – which is not likely to be far removed from its trade equilibrium level – it had been allowed to float downwards, the deficit would have continued because of the delay in the effect of the devaluation on exports of capital goods, and sterling would have become considerably undervalued. The importance of the time-lag between exchange movements and their effect on commercial supply and demand of exchange in the market depends, among other circumstances, on the proportion of capital goods in the foreign trade of the countries concerned. That proportion has increased considerably in the case of Britain, and the resulting increase in the time-lag has further reduced the extent to which adoption of floating exchanges could solve the trade balance problem. For neither exchange rates nor imports and exports stand still during the duration of the time-lag.

We have already alluded to the question of the behaviour of other countries in the face of economic aggression in the form of exchange dumping and import restrictions through exchange depreciation. A much more complicated and even less predictable factor is the extent to which the degree of various elasticities tends to modify the effect of exchange depreciation.

To what extent would supplies of exportable goods and of goods that could replace imports be affected by a depreciation of the exchange? To what extent are imports irreplaceable by home-produced goods, or by goods produced within the same currency area, regardless of their increase of prices caused by the depreciation of the exchange? How would prices in the importing and exporting countries be affected by the depreciation of the exchanges? These are only a few questions which deserve the attention of those supporters of floating exchanges who imagine that the balancing of trade through a depreciation of the exchange is a matter of simple arithmetic.

Some advocates of floating exchanges are alternatively elasticity-optimists and elasticity-pessimists, according to the way in which it happens to suit their argument. The uncertainty of the degree of elasticities and of their effect on the volume and prices of goods exported and imported makes it quite impossible to form even an approximate idea of the extent of the depreciation that would be required to achieve equilibrium. Those responsible for the planning of monetary policy are therefore not in a position to judge whether the game would be worth the candle, among other reasons because they have no means of knowing the size of the candle. They are not in a position to compare the relative advantages and disadvantages of achieving the desired end by means of currency depreciation or by some alternative means. Adoption of floating exchanges is always necessarily a leap in the dark.

This brings us to one of the most important aspects of the controversy, which advocates for floating exchanges have not had the moral courage to face fairly and squarely. They abstain from stating frankly the extent of depreciation of the national currency which they consider to be an acceptable sacrifice for the sake of achieving balance of payments equilibrium. Do they envisage a maximum of 10 per cent, or 50 per cent, or 90 per cent, or even more? Even if economists, politicians outside the Government and other unofficial advocates of floating exchanges can afford to be so irresponsible as to leave this vital point pleasantly vague, those in charge of taking policy decisions must find an answer to this question before taking the plunge.

The role played by leads and lags in the foreign exchange market introduces further complications. It is examined in detail in my *Leads and Lags: The Main Cause of Devaluation.* What matters from the point of view of equilibrium between supply and demand in the foreign exchange market is not the statistical effect of currency depreciation on exports and imports as shown by trade returns, but its effect on the actual supply and demand of foreign exchanges. This depends to a large degree on the way in which currency depreciation affects leads and lags.

The effect of currency depreciation on supply–demand relationship in the foreign exchange market is not a matter of simple arithmetic from this point of view, any more than from the point of view of time-lags or of elasticities. Even if as a result of a certain degree of depreciation imports and exports (including invisible items) come to be balanced statistically, this would not mean that equilibrium would be restored simultaneously in the foreign exchange market. It depends on the changes caused by the depreciation on the length of delays in payments for imports and exports, or, to be precise, on the moment when such payments come to affect the volume of supply and demand in the foreign exchange market.

A depreciation of a currency may shorten or lengthen leads and lags, according to the view of importers and exporters as to whether the movement has gone far enough. If they are satisfied that the exchange has reached its equilibrium level, they may shorten their leads and lags. If they do so prematurely they may hinder the depreciation and delay the completion of the adjustment. If, on the other hand, the depreciation becomes self-aggravating, they might lengthen their leads and lags and the exchange rate might overshoot its equilibrium level.

Even if we were to assume for the sake of argument that the various 'other things' relating to imports and exports, discussed earlier in this chapter, remained unchanged, the equilibrating effect of exchange depreciation would still be liable to be upset by the effect of capital movements, speculation and arbitrage on the supply and demand in the foreign exchange market. Reference was already made to these all-important aspects of the subject in the last chapter, and they will be examined in greater detail in the next three chapters.

The wide variety of invisible imports and exports is apt to respond to exchange depreciation in various ways. For instance, if a country has very large debts or claims abroad in terms of foreign currencies, the burden of the debt service in terms of the national currency would increase in proportion to the depreciation of the national currency. This would not affect its invisible imports or exports. If the country has large claims or debts in terms of its own currency, its invisible exports or imports represented by receipts or payments would change in terms of foreign currencies, so that its balance of payments would be affected to that extent.

There is yet another aspect of the effect of currency depreciation on the trade balance. A trade deficit increases the volume of goods available in the home market and tends to keep down the rise in prices, especially as increased foreign competition tends to induce some home shoppers to try to keep their costs down. A reduction of the trade deficit resulting from a depreciation of the exchange tends to accentuate the rise in prices, not only because it means a reduction in the volume of goods available for meeting domestic demand, but also because under the protection of an appreciation of foreign exchanges local manufacturers can well afford to charge higher prices for their goods and to relax their resistance to wage claims and to other increases in their costs.

Over and above all, the abandonment of the defence of the parity would enable the Government to increase its expenditure, relax the squeeze and abandon such effort as it has made towards enforcing an incomes policy. This alone would be sufficient to accentuate the rise in prices. The result would be that part of the effect of the depreciation on the volume of exports and imports would be cancelled out. More would be consumed at home and less would be exported. The downward floating of the exchange rate would be to that extent self-defeating. It would have to float much further downwards to offset the various adverse effects of its depreciation on imports and exports than it was expected to have on the basis of the price level existing before the beginning of its downward movement.

CHAPTER EIGHT

Balancing and Unbalancing Capital Movements

IN an ideal world import surpluses and export surpluses would be balanced all the time automatically by long-term capital movements in the opposite sense. Consequently trade imbalance would not alter the *status quo* in respect of the size of the reserves or of the balance of international short-term indebtedness. Nor would exchange rates be affected by surpluses and deficits, except temporarily in a somewhat less ideal world in which it would be difficult to synchronise trade deficits and surpluses with long-term capital movements in the opposite sense, so that there might be surplus supply or demand in the market during the time-lag.

In our real world, capital movements may or may not tend to balance trade surpluses or deficits in the long run, but they tend to be an unbalancing factor in the short run, exaggerating an imbalance in foreign trade and in current payments in general. Even when the capital movements are in the right direction, there is no reason why their extent should just suffice to offset international payments arising from trade surpluses or other sources either in the short run or in the long run. The fact that some nations had become creditor nations and others debtor nations over periods of decades and even centuries proves that there are no built-in influences in operation to ensure that capital movements must tend to balance international accounts even in the long run. And the fact that countries with floating or highly flexible exchanges – such as several Latin American countries have been most of the time – tend to increase their international indebtedness simultaneously with the depreciation of their currencies conclusively proves that capital movements need not be a balancing item except in a purely book-keeping sense, in the same way as two sides of a balance sheet are always bound to add up to the same figure.

In examining the effect of exchange movements on capital imports and exports, we must discriminate between short-term and long-term capital movements. Within the category of long-term capital movements we must distinguish between direct investments and portfolio investments. Within the category of short-term capital movements we must distinguish between covered and uncovered transactions.

There is no reason whatsoever for assuming that changes in exchange rates tend automatically to influence long-term capital movements (*a*) towards achieving equilibrium between capital imports and exports or (*b*) towards balancing surpluses or deficits on current trading account in general and on foreign trade in particular. It is of course conceivable that a country which strictly controls its capital movements might achieve that end over a period of time. What matters is that there is no built-in balancing influence in a free or comparatively free economy that would tend to produce that effect.

We saw in the last chapter that, even in the absence of non-commercial influences tending to divert exchange rates from the level at which imports and exports would balance, the contention that if exchange rates were allowed to take care of themselves they would settle at their trade equilibrium level is utterly untenable. But it must be admitted that there is at any rate a distinct tendency for the quantity of imports to decline and for that of exports to increase when an exchange is depreciating, even if that tendency is liable to be interfered with by a variety of cross-currents. As far as long-term capital movements are concerned, however, no such tendency exists at all.

Admittedly capital movements arising from direct investments or foreign portfolio investments abroad might be affected by exchange movements in given circumstances. A substantial overvaluation of the currency of a capital-exporting country in terms of the currency of a capital-importing country is liable to induce the former country to 'pick up bargains' by taking over firms in the latter country at low prices. Likewise the anticipation of a substantial revaluation or appreciation of a currency might influence the decision of industrial concerns abroad to acquire capital assets in the country with a revaluation-prone currency, even though against the prospects of a once-for-all capital gain the effects of a revaluation on the competitive capacity of the firm to be taken over have to be taken into consideration.

But decisions to export capital in the form of direct investment are liable to be affected by so many considerations that are independent of the position or prospects of the exchange rates – availability and cost of investment capital, attitude of the two Governments concerned, labour conditions, the existence or extent of xenophobia, relative extent and nature of taxation, the nature of legislation affecting business concerns in general and foreign firms in particular, political stability, to mention only a few – that the extent of the undervaluation of the currency concerned must be very considerable to determine the decisions. Views taken by investors on the prospects of devaluation-prone exchanges of the capital-importing countries are liable to discourage direct investment, unless hedging against the exchange risk on the investment is possible and not unduly costly.

Similar considerations apply to decisions in respect of disinvestment, with the additional influence of the natural reluctance of firms with direct investments abroad to withdraw their investments from the country with a devaluation-prone currency. A decision to disinvest might be even more difficult than a decision whether to invest or abstain from investing. It may be influenced by exchange movements, but also by a multitude of other considerations.

It is evident from the above observations that as far as movements of capital through direct investment are concerned, there can be no such thing as an equilibrium rate of exchange at which investments and disinvestments in both directions should automatically tend to balance. Nor is it conceivable that there might be an exchange rate at which net direct investments or net direct disinvestments would offset the surplus or deficit on current trading account or on current payments account. Such a result could only be produced in a totalitarian economy based on strict bilateralism. Indeed international movements of capital are even liable to 'flow uphill' systematically. Residents in a country with a trade deficit and a depreciating exchange as well as non-residents holding investments in that country have a strong inducement to transfer their capital to some other country. This is especially the case if that country is subject to social or political troubles. Capital movements connected with direct investment are liable to aggravate the trade deficit instead of offsetting it.

Notwithstanding exchange controls, there is from time to time much flight of capital from a country the exchange of which is depreciating or is expected to depreciate through a trade deficit, to countries the exchanges of which are appreciating or are expected to appreciate through a trade surplus. But expectations of changes in exchange rates are by no means the only influence affecting such movements – very often not even the most important influence.

The position is roughly similar in respect of portfolio investments, with the difference that they are more mobile than direct investments. Considerations of exchange rates are more likely to influence capital movements in that form. This does not mean, however, that such considerations need to be decisive, nor that they tend to influence investment decisions in an equilibrating sense. Considerations of risks, of a kind that cannot be hedged against by forward exchange operations, are liable to outweigh the prospects of capital gains or of higher yields resulting from foreign exchange appreciation.

For all these reasons, and for many others, it is utterly unlikely that an exchange could float to a level at which supply and demand in the foreign exchange market arising from movements of long-term capital would necessarily balance as a result of the change in the exchange rate. Nor is there any reason to expect that such movements would ever offset an import surplus or an export surplus except by sheer coincidence. But if the unexpected should ever happen, it would obviate the necessity for the exchange rate to float to a level at which imports and exports would balance independently of capital movements. For supply and demand in the foreign exchange market would balance in spite of the continued existence of an import surplus or an export surplus.

Such a coincidence is, however, as likely to occur under a system of fixed exchange rates as under a system of floating exchange rates. Something like it did in fact occur, broadly speaking, in the experience of the United States in 1968 when the balance of payments deficit on current account was more or less offset by borrowing abroad. The removal of the peg would not increase the remote chance of the imbalance on account of trade being offset by an imbalance in the opposite sense on capital account.

An exchange rate which would balance imports and exports of goods and services would be most unlikely to balance also the import and export of long-term capital. In any case many kinds of long-term capital movements are not affected by movements of exchange rates in a balancing sense, and some of them are affected in an unbalancing sense. If for no matter what reason imports and exports of long-term capital remain unbalanced at the exchange rate at which the trading account balances, the resulting discrepancy between supply and demand in the foreign exchange market would tend to divert exchange rates from their trade equilibrium level, quite apart from any possible imbalance on speculative or arbitrage account.

Movements of short-term capital depend mainly on interest differentials, allowing for the forward margin if the exchange risk is covered, and on the view taken of the prospects of the exchange if the exchange risk is not covered. Transfers of uncovered funds constitute a form of speculation and will therefore be discussed in detail in the next chapter, which deals with that subject. Transfers of covered funds will be dealt with in Chapter 10 on arbitrage.

If the exchange risk is covered, the trend of the flow of balances and of short-term transactions by banks depends on the interplay between interest differentials and forward rates, subject to limitations of funds available for interest arbitrage and for foreign credits. It is also affected by views taken on the possibility of change in the exchange control measures and views taken about political and commercial risks. Movements of covered short-term capital need not be affected by a depreciation of the spot exchange, though a self-aggravating depreciating trend of the spot rate might foreshadow the possibility of exchange control. In such circumstances movements of covered balances, so far from tending to reduce an imbalance on trading account, are apt to increase it.

The behaviour of long-term and short-term capital movements described above completely invalidates the theory on which the advocacy of floating exchanges is based – that exchanges, if left to themselves, tend to drift towards trade equilibrium level at which imports and exports of goods and services balance. Confronted with the incontrovertible fact that capital movements are affected by a different set of influences from those affecting the movement of goods, advocates of that theory have marshalled up an impressive array of arguments trying to prove close relationship between capital movements and interest rates, prices and other factors that are liable to affect imports and exports. They contend vaguely that in the long run capital movements assist in the equalisation of imports and exports.

But then, in the long run we are all dead. Even if we were to assume, for the sake of argument, that capital movements affect imports and exports in an equilibrating sense after a time-lag of as short as, say, three months, they would be of little use from the point of view of keeping the exchange rates at the level at which imports and exports balance. For during the intervening period the imbalance in capital movements would tend to divert exchange rates from trade equilibrium level and, as a result, imports and exports would also be affected. Long-run balancing of capital movements would only help if exchange rates stood still at their equilibrium level, pending the effect of balancing capital movements on exchanges. Since that is most unlikely, the efforts to prove the indirect effect of changes in the imbalance between imports and exports on capital movements, impressive as they are to those who want to believe in the argument, are irrelevant.

Suppose the exchange rate at which imports and exports would tend to balance is $2.20. If at the time when sterling has floated down to that level there is a deficit on capital account, sterling would continue to depreciate below $2.20 in spite of the cessation of the trade deficit. This would unbalance imports and exports. For the purposes of foreign trade sterling would become undervalued, and the result would tend to be an export surplus. That in itself would not matter. But since in the meantime domestic prices and wages in Britain would adapt themselves to the lower exchange rate of sterling, when supply and demand in the market on capital account becomes balanced sterling would appreciate, conceivably above its lowered trade equilibrium level.

If there is a surplus on capital account it prevents sterling from depreciating to its trade equilibrium level. The resulting prolongation of the overvaluation of sterling would tend to prevent the balancing of imports and exports. A depreciation of the exchange does not automatically correct the surplus on capital account even to the extent to which it tends to correct the deficit on current account.

There is in practice no equilibrium rate at which capital movements would necessarily balance. They are only remotely and incompletely affected by the current trade balance and by exchange rates. It is virtually inconceivable that they would happen to balance at the rate at which trade also tends to balance. This means that in all probability the rate at which trade balances would leave supply and demand in the foreign exchange market unbalanced on capital account. To balance them, the exchange rate would tend to shift to a level at which trade would cease to balance.

CHAPTER NINE

Speculative Deviations

EVEN if, through sheer coincidence bordering on miracle, the inflow and outflow of capital happened to balance at the exchange rate at which imports and exports are at equilibrium, it would not follow at all that the exchange rate would necessarily become adjusted to its trade equilibrium level and would settle down around it. For there are also the speculation and arbitrage factors to reckon with. This chapter is concerned with the former.

It is of course tempting for those engaged in constructing a model based on the assumption that floating rates would adjust themselves automatically to their trade equilibrium level to disregard the possibility of speculative deviations from that level. They may convince themselves and may try to convince others that if supply and demand of foreign exchanges is balanced both on trade account and on capital account, there is no inducement for engaging in speculative operations, for no further exchange movements are expected. This argument is invalid even from a purely theoretical point of view.

No advocate of floating rates, however completely divorced from reality, has the right to assume that, once the rates have reached a level at which trade and capital movements are balanced, it would remain stable at that level for ever. Since import–export relationship as well as the relationship between capital imports and exports would never be rigidly fixed, the ideal theoretical equilibrium rate would itself be subject to changes. Such changes might be quite considerable from time to time. There would be no rigid stability, but a continuous process of readjustment to the ever-changing parities. Seasonal discrepancies would still arise between imports and exports.

The domestic price levels in the countries concerned and the ratio between them would be subject to changes. Long-term capital movements could not possibly offset from day to day or even from week to week or month to month discrepancies arising from any such changes. Offsetting short-term capital movements would have to be induced by changes in exchange rates. Any such changes, or prospects of changes, would be liable to be anticipated by speculation.

Even if trade and capital movements could achieve perfect static equilibrium, there would be innumerable reasons for which speculative operations would be liable to develop. Operators may anticipate political troubles, or Government measures likely to affect exchange rates, or a bad harvest, or a major strike, or one of the hundreds of other changes in the situation or prospects at home or abroad that are liable to affect exchange rates.

When all or most speculators take the same view, the resulting one-sided pressure on the exchange moves the rate until it reaches a level at which the closing of speculative positions, or the initiation of speculative operations in the opposite sense, would bring the movement to a standstill. Speculative buying and selling would then become balanced at an equilibrium level which would almost certainly differ from the equilibrium level for trade and the one for capital movements. There is no reason to suppose that the long arm of coincidence, thanks to which trade and capital movements might by some miracle balance at the same rate, would lengthen to such fantastically abnormal extent as to make the equilibrium rate for speculative operations coincide with both the equilibrium rate for trade and the equilibrium rate for capital imports and exports. If coincidence is not carried that far, speculative trends must divert the exchange rate from the equilibrium level for commercial and capital transactions.

Speculation in foreign exchanges in a narrow sense means deliberate creation of long or short positions in a foreign currency for the purpose of benefiting by an expected change in the exchange rate. In a broader sense it also covers leads and lags – changes in the timing of imports and exports, or of payments for them, or of the covering of the exchange risk on them. In an even broader sense it also covers hedging operations – investment-hedging, by which investors abroad seek to safeguard themselves against losses through the effect of a devaluation of the currency in terms of which they hold their investment, or inventory-hedging by importers against losses on their stocks through a fall in their prices resulting from a devaluation of the exporters' currency. For the purpose of this chapter all foreign exchange operations are considered speculative if they are undertaken in expectation of a profit through changes in the exchange rate.

The main economic justification of speculation in foreign exchanges is that it provides a counterpart for surpluses of buying or selling arising from trade or from capital movements. To the extent to which it fulfils this role it is decidedly constructive – a fact which is not realised by those who would like to do away with speculation altogether. On the other hand, if speculation creates net surplus buying or selling the counterpart for which, in the absence of official intervention, has to be provided – at a price – by speculation in the opposite sense, it plays a decidedly disturbing role. Under fixed parities speculative selling reduces official reserves and/or increases official foreign liabilities until the speculative short positions come to be covered by speculators. Under floating exchanges it causes exchanges to depreciate.

Of course it is convenient for advocates of floating exchanges to be able to tell us that under their system speculation would merely assist exchange movements towards the level at which imports and exports would balance. But there is no shadow of justification for taking such an optimistic view.

Speculative operations are undoubtedly influenced to a very considerable extent by the position and prospects of the balance of payments. But even in the complete absence of any other influences this would not necessarily mean that equilibrium in the balance of payments at a certain exchange rate would also create equilibrium in supply and demand through speculative accounts at the same rate. For one thing, speculators who take a certain view about the balance of payments position and prospects have no means of knowing whether any prevailing exchange rate corresponds to the level at which exports and imports balance each other. They have no means of knowing for some time whether or not exports and imports are balanced at any given moment. There is bound to be a time-lag before the trade returns become available, and in the meantime the picture may have changed considerably. In Britain this time-lag is about a fortnight – a quite unnecessarily long delay – after the end of each month as far as visible trade is concerned. The fact that trade returns for, say, April show imports and exports evenly balanced does not necessarily exclude the possibility that it would become unbalanced once more by the middle of May. Indeed the situation is liable to change very considerably from week to week. And it is of no use arguing that such short-term changes do not matter and that, for the purposes of the satisfactory operation of floating exchanges, all that would matter is that the exchange rate should fluctuate around a level at which trade would balance over a period of, say, three or six months. Any surpluses or deficits within that period might be disregarded from a theoretical point of view. But from a practical point of view they could not be disregarded, since they would divert the exchange rate from its trade equilibrium level. Such diversions, even for a few weeks, and certainly for a few months, might be sufficient to unbalance trade or to initiate a self-aggravating trend in the exchange rate.

In any case trade returns are very far from being an exact science; their figures are far from being complete and are most undependable. Moreover, reliable information about some items of invisible imports and exports is non-existent, and in any case the time-lag before the publication of such calculations as can be made relating to them is longer than for the publication of statistics on visible imports and exports. Meanwhile we have to be content with 'guesstimates'. Nor are there sufficiently up-to-date figures on international capital movement, the current figures for which are liable to exaggerate the effect of any discrepancies between commercial transactions on exchange rates and to divert exchange rates from their trade equilibrium levels.

For these reasons alone balanced trade and balanced capital movements would certainly not rule out major discrepancies between speculative buying and selling of foreign exchanges. Nor would equilibrium of commercial and capital transactions mean absence of speculative operations. Even if speculators were wrong about their assessment of the state of the balance of payments, operations resulting from their mistaken judgement would nevertheless tend to divert the exchange rate from the level at which imports and exports would offset each other.

It is always largely a matter of opinion whether the trade balance may be considered to be at equilibrium, so that one can never be certain whether the prevailing rate really corresponds to trade equilibrium level. If, rightly or wrongly, speculators don't think so, their operations could cause the exchange rate to move to a level at which trade would no longer be at equilibrium even if it was balanced before speculators took a hand. The volume of disequilibrating speculative operations is apt to be very large at times, so that exchange rates are apt to be diverted by them from their trade equilibrium levels to a very considerable extent. On the other hand, in many situations equilibrium would be reached in the foreign exchange market, as a result of speculative operations, at rates which differ considerably from the trade equilibrium level. This might mean that the depreciation of a freely floating exchange is halted before the level is reached at which imports and exports would balance. Or it might mean that the depreciation continues after the trade equilibrium level is reached and supply and demand in the market come to be balanced at an undervalued rate. Such situations are liable to arise if speculators are unduly optimistic or pessimistic about the balance of payments position or outlook.

Admittedly, speculative operations would often tend to

assist exchange rates to reach trade equilibrium level under a floating system. As often as not, however, they are liable to operate in an unbalancing sense. Even if speculation is pressing the exchange in the same direction as commercial influences, by aggravating the selling pressure due to a trade deficit it is liable to bring the rate to its theoretical trade equilibrium level prematurely, before a more moderate degree of depreciation would have produced its full effect on imports and exports. If speculators were omniscient they might realise when exactly the exchange reaches equilibrium in the absence of other disturbing influences and they might act upon their knowledge. But they are in an even worse position to know the whereabouts of the equilibrium level than the authorities, and they are in a much worse position to know whether trade is in fact balanced.

Advocates of the floating system work on the assumption that the weighted average views of all those concerned with foreign exchanges would produce the ideal rate. In reality if such a weighted average could ever correspond to the equilibrium rate it would be sheer coincidence. If the foreign exchange market consisted of a computer into which all buying and selling orders coming from every source were to be fed, the outcome would be the ideal rate in the sense that the weighted average of buying and selling orders would truly represent supply–demand relationship. But the effect of supply and demand has to operate through the intermediary of human minds and not through an electronic mechanism. This means that the outcome is affected by the human factor. The response to identical changes in supply–demand relationship is apt to differ widely according to the way in which a large number of human minds reacts to them. This consideration alone should be sufficient to cast doubt on the theory, which is based upon the mechanical concept of the foreign exchange market.

Speculative influences, by causing exchanges to deviate considerably from their trade equilibrium level, would play a much more disturbing role under floating exchanges than they play under stable exchanges. Under fixed parities speculators are apt to operate both ways, as many of them are inclined to expect the authorities to be able to maintain existing parities. It is only when a really strong feeling develops in the market about the imminence of a devaluation or a revaluation that speculators all turn one way, as they did on the eve of the devaluation of sterling in 1967. Under floating rates, on the other hand, even influences and events of relatively small importance, which under fixed parities would not give rise to expectations of changes in parities, would be sufficient to trigger off strong speculative trends in exchange rates in anticipation of their unrestrained effect on the floating exchange rate.

Although under fixed parities occasional devaluations or revaluations are apt to cause major changes in the economic system, similar troubles are liable to occur much more frequently under floating rates, after each major movement, and their extent is apt to be more considerable. While the extent of changes in parities is nowadays usually kept down to a minimum, there is virtually no limit to exaggerated exchange movements under floating rates. Better prospects of bigger profits would attract additional sets of speculators who would not take a hand in waves of speculative operations under fixed parities – this in spite of the bigger risk attached to speculation under floating exchanges.

Having regard to the above, it seems reasonable to assume that, as a result of speculative exaggerations of exchange movements, the extent of imbalance liable to develop under floating exchanges would be larger than that of the imbalance developing under fixed parities. It is true, fixed parities prevent exchanges from adapting themselves to their trade equilibrium levels. But the ease with which overvalued currencies suddenly become undervalued or vice versa shows that in reasonably normal conditions the extent of disequilibrium is usually relatively moderate. Throughout the 'fifties and until 1964 sterling fluctuated fairly near its trade equilibrium level, thanks to the policy of stop–go pursued by the Conservative Governments.

It was the abandonment of that policy by the Labour Government that resulted in a chronic overvaluation of sterling until its devaluation in 1967. It was, and still is, widely believed that the moderate devaluation by 14 per cent restored the balance between prices in Britain and abroad.

Under floating rates speculative movements would not stop short at anything like 14 per cent. Deviations of exchanges from their trade equilibrium level would be much more pronounced because of the self-aggravating character of speculative drives. The influence of frequently recurrent wide fluctuations on the economy would be much stronger than that of more moderate and infrequent changes of parities. Speculators would be given immense power to damage the economies of the countries adopting that system and also the economies of other countries which would also be exposed to exaggerated undervaluations or overvaluations of their own currencies resulting from the wide movements of floating exchanges. The Governments would simply hand over to the 'gnomes' their power to determine exchange rates.

CHAPTER TEN

The Dynamism of Arbitrage

In earlier chapters we examined the disturbing dynamism of intervals between changes in exchange rates and their effect on imports and exports, of leads and lags, of capital movements and of speculation. Our next task is to investigate the disturbing dynamism of arbitrage. On the face of it the suggestion that arbitrage transactions are liable to divert exchange rates from the level at which imports and exports would balance may appear to be paradoxical. For the essence of arbitrage is that it does not alter supply–demand relationship. Nevertheless it is my contention that exchange arbitrage transactions of every kind – whether space arbitrage, time arbitrage or interest arbitrage – are liable to affect exchange rates and might interfere with their tendency to settle around their trade equilibrium levels.

Even space arbitrage, which merely aims at taking advantage of discrepancies between quotations in different markets at a given moment, and which merely shifts surplus supply or surplus demand from one market to another, is liable to affect exchange rates – this in spite of the fact that it does not alter the grand total of supply or the grand total of demand arising from commercial transactions, capital movements or speculative transactions. In normal conditions space arbitrage has an equilibrating effect. But in nervous markets, and even more in disorderly markets, it is liable to generate or exaggerate upward or downward trends.

It is true, thanks to the remarkable improvement of the mechanism of the foreign exchange market since the war, all the free markets now may be said to constitute one vast international market. It is just as easy today to transact foreign exchange business across the Channel or across the Atlantic as across the two sides of Old Broad Street. All transactions – except those carried out in certain continental markets where foreign exchange dealers meet in the flesh for a brief session every day – are carried out with the aid of telephone or teleprinter, and delays in long-distance communications are now quite exceptional. In theory, therefore, the shifting of an overspill of demand for dollars, say, from Paris to London, should not make any difference whatsoever to the overall tendency of the exchange rate or to the strength of that tendency. In practice, however, situations are liable to arise in which arbitrage in space does affect exchange rates.

London is easily the best market in dollars. Continental banks often prefer to deal with London banks when large amounts are involved, because such operations are less likely to move the rate against them. Or they undo in London large commitments that were originally assumed locally or in relation to some other continental centre. In order to buy spot dollars in London they would have to buy sterling simultaneously, so that aggregate buying pressure and aggregate selling pressure on sterling increase to an equal extent and offset each other. But if Paris buys spot dollars in London on a large scale, the result of such operations is an appreciation of the dollar against sterling and a depreciation of the French franc against sterling.

Owing to the outstanding importance of the sterling–dollar rate, a decline of the sterling–dollar rate is liable to produce an unfavourable psychological effect on sterling, even though it appreciates at the same time against the franc. Under fixed parities the extent of this influence is liable to remain limited, owing to the operation of the support points mechanism. The French authorities would be supporting the franc if, as a result of selling pressure on it in London, it reaches its minimum support point in relation to the dollar, or even at an earlier stage. The British authorities would be supporting sterling. The technique of the support points mechanism under fixed parities is described in detail in my *Textbook on Foreign Exchange*.

Under floating rates, however, a purely technical movement arising from triangular arbitrage is liable to go far in the absence of official intervention. A sudden increase of demand for dollars in London on French account, arising from an appreciation of the dollar as a result of a big buying order in the much narrower Paris market and from the resulting space arbitrage operations between Paris and London, is liable to affect the sterling–dollar rate in given circumstances. If the undertone of sterling is weak, French selling of sterling against dollars in London is apt to accentuate its weakness. The extent of its effect is liable to be relatively strong if even before the advent of this new pressure the trend in London was already one-sided. In given circumstances, its self-aggravating effect is liable to affect the discrepancy between the actual exchange rate and the equilibrium rate for trade. It may play an unbalancing role in preventing the exchange rate from adjusting itself to its equilibrium level. Admittedly, in normal circumstances that effect would be negligible. But if it occurs at a moment when sterling has a weak undertone, it might exaggerate the movement to an appreciable extent.

Time arbitrage, like space arbitrage, serves the purpose of eliminating discrepancies, not between different markets – unless it is combined with space arbitrage – but between quotations of forward rates for different maturities at any given moment. Like space arbitrage, it does not directly affect the aggregate volume of supply of or demand for foreign exchanges, or the discrepancy between them. Its obvious effect is that it influences differences between rates quoted for various maturities, as expressed in percentages per annum. What is less obvious is its possible effect on the trend of spot rates. For instance, heavy pressure on short forward rates resulting from time arbitrage is liable to produce a strong effect on those rates. In given circumstances it is liable to produce strong psychological reactions or to reinforce existing psychological reactions, which is liable to affect spot rates.

Changes in forward rates for certain maturities caused by time arbitrage are also liable to react on the supply–demand relationship of Euro-currencies and on Euro-currency rates. This again tends to influence the spot rates. Finally, to the extent to which time arbitrage affects forward rates for three months, the most important maturity for trade, it influences the exchange rates which must conform to trade equilibrium level in order that imports should be balanced by exports. As in the case of space arbitrage, the effect might be balancing or unbalancing, according to whether it tends to widen or to narrow the discrepancy between spot rates and their trade equilibrium level.

Uncovered interest arbitrage constitutes short-term capital movements and is of a speculative character. Covered interest arbitrage does not result in capital movements, but only to the exchange of capital in terms of one currency against capital in terms of another. It only results in capital movements if it is combined with a short-term deposit or investment transaction. Otherwise it is, as its name implies, just a 'swap' of one currency against another. But the fact that neither side becomes a debtor or a creditor does not necessarily mean that swap transactions do not affect the supply–demand relationship in the foreign exchange market. One of the two parties is more likely to sell the foreign currency he obtained for a limited period than is the other. It depends on the degree of confidence in the currencies and on the aim of the operations.

If sterling is under a cloud, the bank that has bought spot sterling against the sale of forward sterling might sell the spot sterling, thereby creating a short position. On the other hand the bank that bought spot dollars against the sale of forward dollars keeps the dollars for the duration of the contract. The resulting selling pressure on spot sterling is liable to affect the discrepancy between the actual rate and the trade equilibrium rate. The effect can be in a balancing sense or in an unbalancing sense. What matters from the point of view with which we are here concerned is that covered interest arbitrage is liable, in given circumstances, to divert the actual exchange rate from trade equilibrium level, even though in different circumstances it might contribute towards the adjustment of the actual rate to the trade equilibrium level.

Covered interest arbitrage is liable to affect the spot rate of a depreciation-prone currency unfavourably. For the role that swap transactions play is to divert selling pressure from the forward exchange rate to the spot exchange rate. If as a result of a speculative attack on sterling the discount on forward sterling widens, it might become profitable for those who do not expect a depreciation of sterling to transfer funds from London to New York with the forward exchange covered. This tends to offset the effect of the adverse pressure on forward sterling at the expense of increasing the adverse pressure on spot sterling. It is true that, as pointed out above, forward rates for three months are important for trade. But they are not so important as spot rates, especially from a psychological point of view. The relationship between spot and forward rates is a highly technical aspect of our subject which is dealt with in detail in my *Dynamic Theory of Forward Exchange*.

As already observed, advocates of floating exchanges do not make it clear whether it is spot rates or forward rates that are expected to become automatically adjusted to equilibrium level. Even under the system of fixed parities forward rates are free to fluctuate beyond support points, unless there is official intervention to maintain them at an artificial level – as forward sterling was maintained between 1964 and 1967 – or unless there is confidence in the maintenance of spot rates at support points.

Presumably advocates of floating rates assume that once the spot rate has settled around its trade equilibrium level, forward margins would settle around their interest parities – the differential between interest rates in the two countries concerned or on the two Euro-currencies concerned. Even if it were so, interest differentials are liable to result in very substantial premiums or discounts on forward exchanges. If there is an interest differential of, say, 4 per cent p.a. and the spot rate is settled around its trade equilibrium level, then the forward rate is at some distance from trade equilibrium level. Since a very high proportion of foreign trade is covered with the aid of forward exchange transactions, from the point of view of those importers and exporters who cover the exchange risk it is the forward rate and not the spot rate that matters. Even though the spot rate might be at a level at which exports are not competitive, if the forward rate of the exporting country's currency is at a substantial discount those exports become competitive before the spot rate depreciates to trade equilibrium level.

It is of course arguable that in normal conditions forward rates are supposed to represent the difference between the cost of financing the transaction in the importing centre and in the importer's currency or in the exporting centre and in its currency or, as the case may be, in the centre or the currency of a third centre or a third currency. But owing to the multiplicity of short-term financing and short-term investment facilities there is not one interest parity for each maturity but a multiplicity of alternative interest parities. Besides, conditions are seldom normal. Forward margins are liable to be diverted from their interest parities by a variety of influences. For a detailed examination of this aspect of the subject I must refer the reader again to my *Dynamic Theory of Forward Exchange*.

Those who are tempted to favour floating rates in the hope that spot rates would become adjusted to their trade equilibrium levels should realise the possibility of abnormal discrepancies between spot and forward rates and between forward margins and their respective interest parities. Such discrepancies might delay the adjustment of spot rates to their trade equilibrium levels or they might divert spot rates from their trade equilibrium levels. On the other hand, in different circumstances they might produce the tendency that steps up the process of adjustment. However this may be, the possibility of the operation of this influence in a disturbing sense should not be overlooked. Those in favour of floating rates should make it plain that the exchange rates which they expect to depreciate or appreciate to trade equilibrium level are either the spot rates or the forward rates or rates that are somewhere between spot and forward rates.

If a currency is floating downwards towards its trade equilibrium level, it is probable that speculative operations tend to accelerate its downward movement. The effect of speculation on forward rates might give rise to outward interest arbitrage which increases pressure on the spot rate but relieves pressure on the forward rate. This aspect of interest arbitrage provides an instance to show that if the argument on floating exchange rises above superficial oversimplification, it is liable to become extremely involved. The idea that advocates convey, deliberately or otherwise, that adjustment of exchange to trade equilibrium rates is a matter of simple arithmetic, is utterly false.

CHAPTER ELEVEN

Self-Aggravating Movements of Floating Rates

IN the foregoing chapters I sought to prove that built-in differences between the trade equilibrium level of exchange rates and their equilibrium levels on other accounts make it impossible for a floating exchange rate ever to settle around its trade equilibrium level. In order that an exchange should behave in accordance with the expectations of those favouring floating exchanges, it would not be sufficient if it adjusted itself to a level at which the import surplus or the export surplus disappeared. There is a continuous process of adjustment of the exchange to the ever-changing pattern of the four equilibrium levels. The object of the present chapter is to show that under the system of floating exchanges movements of exchange rates are liable to be self-aggravating to such an extent that, for that reason alone, they could not settle at their trade equilibrium levels.

There are built-in influences in the system of floating exchanges, making for the development of a disorderly market with strong one-sided buying or selling trends making for exaggerated exchange movements to attract the necessary counterparts to the one-sided buying or selling orders. In such circumstances counterparts are only likely to be forthcoming when the exchange on which there is selling pressure becomes obviously undervalued and when the exchange on which there is buying pressure becomes obviously overvalued. As nobody is in a position to know the whereabouts of the equilibrium rate, the overvaluation or undervaluation would have to assume an exaggerated extent before covering transactions or new operations in the opposite sense would be undertaken on a sufficient scale to restore an orderly market.

If a country adopts the system of floating exchanges, as soon as the peg is removed there is bound to be a rush of speculative and other operations to anticipate the movements of the floating rates. The fact that when the D. mark was temporarily unpegged in September 1969 the rush to buy D. marks was relatively moderate should not lull the responsible authorities into a feeling of complacency in this respect. The D. mark had already been heavily overbought before the suspension of its fixed parity, and besides it was the Government's declared intention to restabilise it as soon as practicable. The probable extent of its eventual revaluation was widely underrated. It would be quite a different story if floating exchanges were adopted for an indefinite period, with no limits, announced or presumed, to their movements. It would also make all the difference if floating exchanges were adopted by a country with a devaluation-prone currency and not by one with a revaluation prone currency. For it is incomparably easier to halt an unwanted appreciation than an unwanted depreciation.

One of the reasons why movements of floating rates would be liable to overshoot their equilibrium level would be the declared intention of the Government concerned not to intervene in the market to influence the movement in progress. Its 'neutrality' might even go so far as to refrain from trying to check the movement by means of conventional monetary policy devices. Indeed one of the attractions of the system, in the eyes of its advocates, is precisely that it would obviate the necessity for adopting conventional monetary measures in order to resist the movement of the exchange.

Under the system of fixed exchanges many operators are prepared most of the time to rely on the official support points and expect the Government, by borrowing abroad, to be able to intervene effectively in order to prevent exchange movements from depreciating or appreciating beyond them. Under a system of floating exchanges it is clearly understood that the Government's policy is to keep strictly aloof from the foreign exchange market and even to abstain from credit squeeze and incomes freeze in defence of the exchange rate. There would be no need for speculators to restrain their operations for fear that they might be caught out by unexpected official intervention.

Any strong trend which is in progress in the foreign exchange market is liable to become exaggerated as result of the market-mentality which expects the prevailing movement to continue. It is not likely to stop and become reversed spontaneously until its exaggerated extent comes to be sufficiently widely realised by the market and by those outside the market whose transactions give rise to buying or selling in the market.

What advocates of floating exchanges refuse to realise adequately is that under the system of their choice the equilibrium level at which they hope that the exchange would settle is liable to shift as a direct result of the very same exaggerated exchange movements that are likely to occur when exchanges are allowed to float freely. Under a system of fixed exchanges the equilibrium level changes through differences between domestic economic trends in various countries or, if the trends are in the same direction, through differences in their respective degrees. Under the floating exchanges differences between domestic economic trends due to influences confined to the particular countries are of course just as likely to occur as under fixed rates. But the equilibrium level is liable to change not only through such differences but, in addition, also as an inevitable result of the major exchange movements which could not occur under fixed exchanges. Even if the exchange rates merely tended to become adjusted to the existing trade equilibrium level, their movements in that direction are themselves liable to bring about a change in the equilibrium level.

For instance, if sterling tended to depreciate to a level at which imports and exports tend to balance this depreciation itself would tend to cause a further increase of prices and wages in Britain. Even if the depreciation is caused by the high relative level of wages (allowing for differences in productivity of labour) and of prices compared with those of other countries, the process of adjustment itself would raise wages and prices even higher. Consequently the trade equilibrium level for sterling would become lower than it was before the beginning of the process of its automatic adjustment to its original trade equilibrium level. The new equilibrium level would decline, because of the additional increase in wages and prices that would follow the movement of sterling towards its *previous* equilibrium level as surely as night follows day. If, as a result of speculative influences, or of adverse capital movements, or for no matter what other reasons unconnected with trade, it should depreciate to below its previous equilibrium level, its resulting additional undervaluation would of course tend to cause an additional rise in prices and wages.

It is true, as soon as speculators realise that the depreciation was overdone, a reaction would set in. But since in the meantime the rise in prices and wages caused by the 'temporary' excessive depreciation would have lowered the equilibrium level, a reversal of the speculative trend would tend to cause sterling to recover towards its new lower equilibrium level – not toward its *old* higher equilibrium level.

According to the static theory it is always discrepancies between exchange rates and trade equilibrium level, or changes in the equilibrium level itself, that would take the initiative, and the exchange rate would adapt itself to the equilibrium level. According to the dynamic theory, however, the equilibrium level itself would be exposed to changes not only as a result of influences affecting price levels and wage levels but also as a direct result of the very exchange movements that had been brought about by the discrepancies between exchange rates and trade equilibrium levels. This means that a high degree of self-aggravating dynamism tending to change the equilibrium level itself is inherent in the system of floating rates.

Exaggerated depreciation and its effect on the equilibrium level could only be prevented if the downward adjustment of the exchange to its equilibrium level were accompanied by measures of credit squeeze and other unpopular measures similar to those applied under a system of fixed exchanges. But then one of the main arguments in favour of the system of floating exchanges is precisely the false assumption that under it there would be no need for interfering with economic expansion and prosperity by resorting to such measures.

In theory, exaggerated movements of floating exchange rates are liable to occur in both directions to the same extent. Once the undervaluation of an exchange comes to be realised, the ensuing reaction is also liable to be exaggerated, just as a pendulum swings back in the opposite direction instead of coming to a halt when it reaches its equilibrium point. In practice, however, fluctuation of a floating rate does not work out that way.

Admittedly an appreciation of the exchange above its equilibrium level, and even its appreciation to equilibrium level, tends to cause a decline in the prices of imported goods. But the resulting downward movement of the price level as a whole is likely to be much less pronounced than the upward movement caused by a corresponding extent of depreciation of the exchange. In particular, during a period of high employment and creeping inflation prices are inelastic downwards. Prices are put up with alacrity following on a depreciation of the exchange, but there is usually a much longer time-lag before they are lowered reluctantly following an appreciation of the exchange. And they may not be changed downwards to anything like the same extent as they would be raised as a result of a depreciation of comparable extent.

As for wages, they are elastic upwards when exchanges depreciate but virtually rigid downwards when exchanges appreciate amidst conditions of full employment and creeping inflation. Indeed, André Siegfried in his *England's Crisis* reminded us that even amidst the large-scale unemployment of the inter-war period it had been very difficult to reduce wages in an effort to correct the overvaluation of sterling. In present-day conditions of high employment an appreciation of sterling would be most unlikely to be followed by cuts in wages. They might not even stop wage increases when sterling floated to a higher level, though conceivably prices would decline and the rate of wage increases might slow down. Even if the appreciation of sterling and its resulting overvaluation were to cause a recession, it would not necessarily halt the upward trend of wages immediately, especially in industries which have long-term wage agreements. Having regard to the present balance of power between employers and employees, a recession would have to proceed very far before the relative bargaining strength of the latter became reduced sufficiently to enable employers to resist further wage demands. As for cuts in wages, if attempted in any of the major industries they might cause a general strike. Having regard to all this, costs of production and prices might continue to rise in spite of the overvaluation of sterling, as they did in fact rise throughout its overvaluation during 1964–67. But even the absence of a fall in costs would be sufficient to bring about an import surplus and a relapse of the floating pound. For this reason any recovery of the floating sterling would be short-lived.

Under the system of floating exchanges the pattern of exchange movements would be exaggerated, depreciations followed by partial and temporary appreciations. Each appreciation would be followed by another depreciation, the extent of which would exceed that of the previous depreciation. The equilibrium level itself would decline lower and lower with each depreciation and would only rise partially and temporarily with each appreciation. Any appreciation above the equilibrium level would be temporary, while any depreciation below equilibrium level would tend to be self-perpetuating. The effect of the asymmetry inherent in floating rates is aptly characterised by Triffin as the 'ratchet effect'.

Any speculative depreciation of a floating exchange tends to create its own justification even if it was originally unjustified. Widely fluctuating exchange rates are apt to change their own equilibrium levels instead of merely adapting themselves to existing equilibrium levels. The operation of this principle was clearly discernible during the period of floating exchanges that followed the First World War. Very often depreciations were not a consequence of a decline of their equilibrium levels caused by domestic inflation but their cause. In innumerable instances prices rose largely as a result of a previous exchange depreciation.

Owing to the asymmetry inherent in the system of floating exchanges, especially in prevailing conditions of high employment and creeping inflation, sterling would be condemned to progressive depreciation in stages, which would be interrupted from time to time, but would be resumed after each brief interval of partial recovery. It seems highly probable that, had the system of floating exchanges been adopted in Britain when the foreign exchange market was reopened in 1951, by now the pound would be worth less than a shilling. And it seems equally probable that, should floating exchanges be adopted now, the purchasing power of the pound would decline by 1980 to the equivalent of today's purchasing power of one shilling. Conceivably its exchange rate might be upheld by declines in the domestic value of other floating currencies as a result of a competitive depreciation race leading to leapfrogging currency depreciations. But that would be small comfort for those in Britain with fixed or inelastic incomes. They would share the fate of the victims of a runaway inflation of which Britain has been mercifully spared until now, thanks to her effort to maintain stable exchange rates. In spite of those efforts, the cost of living rose faster since the Second World War than in any comparable period of British history. But the acceleration of its rise would become truly spectacular under floating exchanges.

It has been suggested that, while fixed rates create a false feeling of security, under a system of floating exchanges a depreciation of sterling might produce a favourable moral effect by frightening the public into becoming public-spirited in the same way as it did in 1931. In an introduction to Mr Powell's pamphlet, *Exchange Rates and Liquidity*, the Institute of Economic Affairs goes so far as to claim that fear of continuing depreciation under floating exchanges would impose on politicians a degree of discipline comparable with the discipline imposed on them by dwindling currency reserves under fixed parities. But then the main attraction of floating exchanges is that under it a depreciation of the exchange would not matter a tinker's cuss, so that Governments and the public would not have to submit to any discipline for the sake of preventing it. Propaganda in favour of floating exchanges succeeded in converting many politicians and a large section of public opinion in favour of that irresponsible attitude. Candid admission of the likelihood, and even of the mere possibility, of having to resort to deflationary measures also under floating exchanges might greatly reduce the appeal of that propaganda.

In any case, owing to the debasement of the British character compared with 1931, a depreciation would have to go very far indeed before the politicians and the public would become frightened into imposing and accepting sacrifices for the sake of making a firm stand to prevent a collapse. This subject is dealt with in detail in my book *Decline and Fall? Britain's Crisis in the Sixties*. During recent years the attitude of the British public towards a depreciation of sterling has changed considerably. This is shown by the complete absence of a response of the British public to the devaluations of 1949 and 1967. Since neither of these devaluations produced a disastrous effect, the British public is no longer impressed to any noteworthy extent, if at all, by the possibility of its repetition or of a depreciation of a floating pound. In 1931 it was prepared to accept heavy sacrifices to save sterling from advanced depreciation. What is more, it re-elected with a record majority the Government that had the courage to impose on it the heavy sacrifices. That history is most unlikely to repeat itself today – unless and until the accelerating depreciation of sterling under the system of floating exchanges should come to produce conditions which would jeopardise full employment.

Since 1931 there have been far-reaching changes in the list of priorities of the British public. Considerably less importance is now attached to the external stability of sterling than in 1931. Even threats to the stability of its domestic purchasing power fail to arouse any country-wide fears, because workers are satisfied that wages would rise at least as fast as the cost of living. On the other hand, considerably more importance has come to be attached to the rate of economic growth and of the rise in the standard of living. Above all, the majority of the public has lost interest in anything that does not concern its standard of living directly and obviously.

Those who seriously expect a more public-spirited response by the nation to a heavy fall of sterling under the system of floating exchanges than to a decline in the reserve and to an increase in the external debt under fixed parities have failed to realise this change in the attitude of the nation. Today it seems inconceivable that a depreciation of the floating pound by as much as 50 per cent or more in twelve months would induce the Government of the day to risk the unpopularity of really drastic cuts in public expenditure. Nor would it induce trade unions to accept cuts in wages, or even to renounce or defer further increases, or to agree to remove restrictive practices merely for the sake of saving the pound from an even heavier depreciation. In these changed circumstances the argument in favour of the floating pound that fears of its depreciation might impose discipline on Governments, and might even bring about a desperately needed national regeneration as it did for a short time in 1931, carries absolutely no conviction.

In Germany, where the memories of the great inflation after the First World War are still very much alive even now, a threat of inflation through the adoption of floating exchanges would still be capable of impressing the public in the right way if the D. mark should float downwards.

Paradoxical as it may sound, this explained in part the German Government's reluctance in 1968–69 to revalue the D. mark. Inflation-conscious Germans were inclined to assume that, once the principle that the parity of the D. mark could be tampered with was conceded, it would be liable to become flexible also in a downward direction. On the other hand, since Britain and the United States had no experience in advanced inflation, the threat of a sharp depreciation of the pound or the dollar does not deter economists from advocating a system carrying that risk. The difference between the German and the Anglo-Saxon attitude towards devices making for inflation – such as Special Drawing Rights – and those tending to weaken psychological resistance to inflation, explains in part the difference in their attitude towards floating rates.

The self-aggravating character of depreciation under floating exchanges, and even under too frequently adjusted parities, is liable to be greatly accentuated by leapfrogging competitive currency depreciations. Governments of rival industrial countries, and also of rival raw-material producing countries, are likely to follow each other's example as a matter of deliberate policy. Or they may have to follow each other's example willy-nilly, owing to the effect of the depreciation of other currencies on their economies, and to the demoralising psychological effects of frequent devaluations or advanced depreciations in general. While a co-ordinated all-round realignment of parities would only produce a limited immediate effect on prices, under leapfrogging depreciations or devaluations prices and wages in each country in turn would increase immediately. The difference may be compared with the difference between orderly strategic retreat and the disorderly flight of a routed army.

On the other hand, appreciations of floating exchanges need not be self-aggravating in their effect on other currencies. Even though the appreciation and overvaluation of the D. mark resulted in an export surplus for Britain, the Government was in a position to decide between allowing sterling to benefit by the change and accumulating the proceeds of the export surplus in order to increase her reserves and/or reduce her external debts. In this respect too there is a built-in asymmetry in the system of floating exchanges.

CHAPTER TWELVE

Trying to Win the Last Peace?

DURING and since the First World War political and military leaders in Britain were often criticised on account of their out-of-date policies or strategies which, it was said, may have been suitable for winning the Crimean War or even the Boer War, but were utterly unsuitable for winning the war of 1914. In the Second World War leadership was rightly accused of pursuing certain military strategies and economic policies that might have been suitable for winning the First World War but were utterly inadequate for winning the Second World War. Similarly, many of the economic policies adopted since 1945 were said to have been suitable for winning the peace of 1919–39 but were utterly unsuitable for winning the peace that followed the Second World War.

In our days, Governments, their official advisers, and many providers of unofficial and unsolicited advice appear to think in terms of conditions prevailing between the two world wars rather than in terms of present-day conditions. They seem to work on the assumption that our main problem is still the danger of large-scale unemployment, so that our policies have to be directed against the evil of deflation rather than against that of inflation.

Economic literature between the two world wars was naturally dominated by the then prevailing large-scale unemployment. It was inspired by a strong desire to reduce unemployment to normal proportions. The possibility of removing it altogether did not even occur to most inter-war writers. Economic and monetary theories and policies put forward by the progressive school rightly aimed at the all-important objective of increasing employment and resisting deflation. Reformers were prompted by determination to support any monetary policy that would assist in industrial expansion.

Nevertheless, as we saw in Chapter 5, a by no means negligible proportion of economists – the majority in number if not in weight – was swimming stubbornly against this tide. Maintenance or restoration of monetary stability occupied a more important place in their lists of priorities than achievement of a high degree of employment or even resistance to a further increase in the abnormally large number of unemployed. Many of them preferred to err, if anything, on the safe side, by advocating additional deflation for the sake of making quite sure that monetary stability was not imperilled by inflation. Yet amidst the then existing conditions this was like being afraid of icebergs in the Sahara or of sunstrokes in the Antarctic.

These dogmatists of stability at any price amidst conditions that had called for flexibility were doing their very best to ensure that the peace preceding the Second World War was well and truly lost, not only in the economic sphere but also in the political sphere. Germany's refusal to follow Britain and other countries in allowing the Reichsmark to depreciate was probably the main cause of the disastrous increase in unemployment and for Hitler's success in overthrowing the Weimar Republic. And France's stubborn determination to safeguard the parity of the franc during 1933–36, even at the cost of allowing Hitler to reoccupy and fortify the Rhineland, was probably the main cause of the Second World War. Many leading economists were fanatic deflationists when deflation was the gravest danger and when timely and adequate departures from stability might have mitigated the world-wide mass sufferings caused by deflation.

Today the pendulum has swung very much in the opposite direction. The majority of economists is now clamouring for the adoption of policies which would mean even more inflation, although it is now inflation that is the main danger. They are in favour of adopting the system of floating exchange rates, not for the sake of preventing deflation – in the way it did in the 'thirties – but for the sake of enabling Governments to bring about or tolerate even larger doses of inflation without feeling handicapped by the need to defend their parities. What their attitude amounts to is that they are in favour of the policy which suited pre-war conditions, but which they or their forerunners opposed before the war when it would have mitigated the depression and might even have averted the Second World War. Had it not been for the deflationary crises in the early 'thirties, Hitler might never have gained control over Germany.

What is curious is that, regardless of the fundamental change in the situation, advocates of floating exchanges hope to carry conviction by using arguments which, weighty as they were before the war, are now meaningless. Many books and articles written in the late 'fifties and throughout the 'sixties argue in favour of floating exchanges largely for the sake of being able to secure full employment. Yet in most industrial countries that end has been largely achieved in spite of stability under the Bretton Woods system. Full employment – in the sense that everybody who really wants a job, even at the cost of changing his occupation or his residence, could get one – has been almost continuous in Britain for most of the time since the war. In other industrial centres, too, there has been a high degree of employment.

It may be objected, of course, that in the United States unemployment is still relatively high and that even in Britain it has increased to above half a million since 1967, reaching 600,000 in 1969. But unemployment in the United States in certain districts and among certain classes is structural, and monetary policy could not cure it. In any case American unemployment statistics grossly exaggerate the real extent of unemployment.

As for Britain, interminable delays in building operations and in repair and maintenance work of every kind, due largely to delays in deliveries of manufactured materials, speak for themselves. Practically every resident in the U.K. and every importer of British goods suffer inconvenience through such delays, which occur in spite of the moderate increase in the number of unemployed. The existence of 'bottlenecks' is conclusive evidence of full employment. Most of the unemployed shown by unemployment statistics are either unemployable, are in transit between jobs, are seasonally unemployed, or, above all, are not prepared to change their residence or their occupation for the sake of obtaining employment. Hence the acute scarcities of labour in many industries and in many districts, which exist in spite of the increase in unemployment in other industries and in certain areas. Many employers do not register their requirements at Labour Exchanges, having learnt by experience that it is useless to do so, because the Labour Exchanges are either unable to supply them with workers or they can only supply them with workers who are quite unsatisfactory even by present-day standards. For all practical purposes, in spite of the existence of about 600,000 unemployed in Britain at the time of writing, there is, therefore, still overfull employment, since the number of *registered and unregistered* vacancies is well in excess of the number of those unemployed who are *genuinely* seeking work.

Whatever other arguments the advocates of floating exchanges may put forward in support of their policy, the prewar argument in favour of flexibility of exchanges – that it is essential to be able to depreciate sterling in order to export unemployment – is utterly unrealistic and irrelevant. Those favouring this policy seem to ignore that the problem today is one of scarcity of labour, not lack of employment, and that there is no unemployment to export.

Supporters of the system of floating exchanges also think in pre-war terms when arguing that the rigidity of parities must be done away with for the sake of faster economic growth. That argument may have carried weight before the war when there was in every country a considerable degree of unused productive capacity. Today, however, most industries in Britain and in many other countries work near the limits of their capacity. The reason why they are unable to increase their output right to the limit of their capacity is not lack of demand or lack of financial resources but lack of skilled labour and in many instances also of unskilled labour. The shameless exploitation of the scarcity of labour by the trade unions and its artificial exaggeration through imposing restrictive practices on the community, is largely responsible for the balance of payments crises which make it necessary to adopt measures that slow down expansion.

Before the war a rising trend of prices resulting from a depreciation of the exchange would have stimulated consumer demand and therefore would also have increased production through making possible a better utilisation of productive capacity. Monetary expansion would have facilitated the financing of growth. Today such expansion would stimulate consumer demand to a much higher degree as a result of higher unearned wages, thanks to competition for the scarce manpower. But it would not materially increase the output, because there is very little unused productive capacity available for that purpose. Moreover the increase in the scarcity of labour would change the balance of power even further in favour of the trade unions, and this would result in a further decline in productivity of labour.

To the extent to which faster growth could be achieved through credit expansion, it has already been achieved in a large measure even in the absence of deliberate expansionary Government policies adopted to that end, thanks to the increased efficiency of the new international money market and the Euro-bond market, and the new domestic money markets, such as the market in inter-bank sterling. These institutions have already done a great deal to finance economic growth by increasing the velocity of deposits.

Before the war declining prices were one of the main causes of the chronic depression. Ever since the end of the war we have been experiencing international non-stop creeping inflation, though its degree has varied from country to country. There is now certainly no need for stimulating the rise in prices as there was between the wars. Indeed any policy that would step up the pace of the prevailing inflation would render a grave disservice to mankind.

Many of those who advocate floating exchanges do so not because they want to accelerate the pace of inflation but because they underrate the extent to which the policy of their choice would produce an inflationary effect. But many more of them feel that it would be well worth while to put up with the disadvantages of rising prices for the sake of accelerated growth and of other advantages that floating exchanges are expected to entail.

The irresponsible attitude of politicians is truly expressed by Mr Enoch Powell in his pamphlet on floating exchanges. Mr Powell, while admitting that expansion would accelerate the decline in the purchasing power of the pound, shrugs off this argument by exclaiming: 'And what of it?' He and many others in favour of floating exchanges want to embark upon expansion in the full knowledge that it would aggravate the danger of accelerating the prevailing inflationary trend. They want floating exchanges not because they ignore their disadvantages, but because they believe that the economic advantages and political popularity of accelerated uninterrupted economic growth would outweigh the economic disadvantages and political unpopularity of accelerated rise in the cost of living. They may well be right during the relatively early phases of inflation. But sooner or later a stage would be reached at which the accentuation of inflation would frighten the public into a sharp reaction against those politicians and economists responsible for the evils of runaway inflation brought about by the success of their propaganda in favour of floating exchanges.

In pre-war conditions of large-scale unemployment it might have been possible to make the system of floating exchanges work both ways, at least to some extent, although, as pointed out earlier, even then it was very difficult to enforce wage reductions when sterling was overvalued. Efforts to adjust wages after the return of sterling to its 1914 parity resulted in a series of strikes culminating in the general strike of 1926.

Now that the balance of power is very much in favour of the trade unions, floating exchanges would mean accelerated increase of unearned wages during periods when sterling would be depreciating, and no reductions of wages during periods when sterling would be appreciating. This alone would be sufficient to make sure that amidst conditions prevailing in Britain in the 'seventies floating exchanges would work one-sidedly in an inflationary sense.

Another change compared with pre-war conditions has been the removal of resale price maintenance. As a result of this change, a depreciation of sterling would produce its effect on the price level much more speedily than it did before the war. Under resale price maintenance manufacturers of nationally advertised goods had tried their best to avoid frequent increases in the controlled retail prices of their goods. They resisted wage demands and other increases in their costs, they tried to become more efficient, they cut their profit margins to defer the day when they had to concede defeat by raising their nationally advertised uniform retail prices. Since, however, recent legislation has deprived them of the control over the retail prices of their manufactures, they no longer have anything like the same incentive to keep their costs down for the sake of avoiding increases in retail prices, since they are no longer responsible for what retailers choose to charge to consumers. This means that retailers are now in a position to exploit to the full any inflationary increase in consumer demand by putting up their prices to the maximum the market can bear.

This aspect of the problem is of course completely overlooked by *laisser-faire* dogmatists and also by the general public. Shoppers are delighted when supermarkets cut prices, without realising that, once the existing stocks are exhausted, prices would invariably increase as a result of the higher costs of production.

In pre-war conditions of underemployment a removal of resale price maintenance might have tended to facilitate a downward adjustment of the price level during periods when sterling was overvalued and the economy was depressed. Prices would have responded more readily to a slackening of consumer demand for retailers would have been content with narrower profit margins in order to rid themselves of their unsold stocks. In present-day conditions the removal of resale price maintenance has been one of the major contributory causes of accelerated inflation.

Before the war a depreciation of exchanges meant an increase of employment and of output. Today it would only mean an increase of unearned wages and of prices. Those who argue in favour of floating exchanges are doing their best to impose on the community a policy that might have won the last peace but would be certain to ensure that we lose the present one.

CHAPTER THIRTEEN

Floating into World Slump

In Chapters 6 to 11 we dealt with the theoretical arguments for and against floating exchanges. The conclusion that emerges is that the theoretical case for the system is utterly fallacious and that, even viewed from a theoretical angle, it is entirely untenable. The present chapter investigates an all-important technical aspect of the suggested system. The practical conclusion emerging from this investigation is so overwhelmingly important that it would turn the balance of argument against the adoption of that system even if the balance of theoretical argument were overwhelmingly in its favour.

It is my contention that under floating exchanges situations are liable to arise in which there would be no adequate forward exchange facilities available for meeting legitimate commercial requirements, and the cost of such facilities as would be available would tend to become prohibitive. In such circumstances many importers and exporters, since they would be unable or unwilling to pay the high cost of the covering facilities in so far as they would be available, would prefer to forgo the transaction altogether rather than expose themselves to losses through major exchange movements. The result might well be a sharp contraction in the volume of foreign trade, which might well cause a world-wide slump comparable with the slump of the 'thirties.

Most theoretical supporters of the system of floating exchanges are blissfully oblivious of the practical argument that under that system the demand for forward exchange facilities would increase considerably while the volume of obtainable facilities would dwindle. Those who take notice of the existence of this argument reject it out of hand. Their contention is that, since under floating exchanges the rates would not be so flagrantly out of equilibrium as under fixed exchanges, there would be less need and not more need for forward covering of commercial transactions. Yet the opposite view is held unanimously by those who have practical experience and who know, therefore, what they are talking about – by business firms and by bankers who are familiar with the attitude of their clients engaged in import and export trade. But economists think they know better than the men who are exposed to losses through omission to cover exchange risks, or whose profit margins are too narrow to allow for the increased cost of covering.

Under fixed exchanges the proportion of foreign trade covered by forward exchanges varies according to the degree of confidence in the Government's willingness and ability to maintain the existing parities against selling or buying pressure. Opinions among businessmen are usually divided. The proportion of those who deem it imperative to cover fluctuates widely according to the expectations of a change in parities. During periods of acute devaluation or revaluation scares one-sided pressure assumes spectacular dimensions, but when devaluation or revaluation fears are relatively moderate a great many business firms refrain from covering.

If all importers or exporters were in the habit of covering all the time, then a lengthening of leads and lags by an average of a single month would be apt to wipe out Britain's entire published reserves. The fact that throughout the long period of fixed parities since the war there was hardly ever a scarcity of forward exchange facilities seems to indicate clearly that under fixed parities a high proportion of merchants don't as a rule cover the exchange risk.

There is every reason to believe that under floating exchanges the proportion of business firms who would cover would be much higher than under fixed exchanges. They could never feel secure with uncovered claims or liabilities. Instead of taking limited and calculable risks as under fixed parities, they would take unlimited and incalculable risks if they refrained from covering. They would expose themselves to ruinous losses. The inducement to cover would no longer be tempered by confidence in the Government's willingness and ability to honour the promise not to change the parity. After all, it would be the Government's declared policy to abstain from preventing major fluctuations. The view would be widely held that the extent of possible depreciations would greatly exceed the probable extent of any devaluation under fixed parities. Had sterling been unpegged in 1967 instead of being devalued, it would in all probability have depreciated considerably more than the 14 per cent it lost through its devaluation. This assumption is supported by the fact that since November 1967 spot sterling was at a discount against its new parities most of the time, and forward sterling was almost always at a discount against the dollar and against most other important currencies.

Under a system of floating exchanges even a mild selling pressure would be sufficient to induce importers and exporters to take steps to safeguard their interests. Under fixed parities many people do not expect the Government to dishonour its oft-repeated pledges to defend the exchange. Unless pressure on the exchange becomes virtually irresistible, opinions about the likelihood of a devaluation would remain divided.

Under floating exchanges, on the other hand, it would be the Government's declared policy to abstain from resisting any pressure, even if moderate and easy to resist. There would therefore be much more frequent rushes by importers to cover their commitments. Whenever they would expect – rightly or wrongly – a depreciation, they would hasten to lengthen their leads. Exporters would lengthen their lags – they would defer their exports, or the collection of the proceeds of their exports. The resulting excess of commercial buying of forward exchanges over commercial selling would be greatly reinforced on each occasion by demand for forward exchange facilities for hedging and speculative purposes.

The landslide of demand for foreign exchanges during the

week that preceded the devaluation of sterling in 1967 gave a foretaste of what would happen from time to time under floating exchanges. During those hectic days of November all importers hastened to cover their requirements to the extreme limit of possibility, and every foreign exporter whose goods were invoiced in sterling hastened to sell the proceeds forward while the going was good. At the same time innumerable speculators were going short in sterling and there was also heavy selling on account of investment-hedging and inventory-hedging by non-resident investors and by holders of stocks imported from Britain and from the Sterling Area.

All this was because Mr Callaghan was this time not prepared to repeat once more his oft-repeated disclaimer of any intention to devalue. Had he gone a step further by openly admitting his intention to abandon the defence of sterling at $2.78 before he was ready to act, the flight from the pound would have been, if possible, even more sweeping. Yet under floating exchanges the authorities would actually go further then merely abstaining from denying their intention to abandon the peg at which they support sterling. It would be their openly declared policy to allow sterling to depreciate.

This would mean that each time the view is taken – rightly or wrongly – that a major depreciation is liable to occur, the landslide of November 1967 would repeat itself. It is true, if the cost of going short in sterling were not kept artificially low through official support, many importers might be unable to afford to cover. This would apply especially to the trade in raw materials, the profit margins on which are narrow. The result of abstaining from purchasing such raw materials might well be a slump in a particularly vulnerable sector of the world economy.

The favourite argument put forward by advocates of floating rates is that under that system the trend of covering might tend to be less one-sided because the cat might jump either way. There would be a possibility of making a profit on a long position, or of suffering a loss on a short position as a result of a recovery of an exchange which had depreciated too far. But the chances are that, under floating exchanges as under fixed exchanges, during currency scares the expectations of the overwhelming majority of those concerned with foreign exchange transactions at any given moment would be in the same sense. The result would be widespread self-aggravating selling pressure or buying pressure. Those who maintain that floating rates would be nearer their equilibrium levels than fixed parities simply beg the question. They also overlook the obvious fact that under fixed parities forward rates are not prevented from moving towards their equilibrium levels.

Even under fixed parities opinions on the likelihood of a change in parities are usually divided, and those who do not expect it or do not consider it imminent swim against the tide of the market. Many of those who anticipate a devaluation or a revaluation are liable to change their opinions and undo their covering or hedging arrangements, in which case their operations tend to offset the prevailing trend. Speculators, too, are liable to take their profits or to cut their losses if their expectations change.

While most of the arguments in this chapter and in this book in general deal with expectations of depreciation, widespread expectations of a sweeping upward trend of a floating currency are also liable to cause scarcities of forward exchange facilities, similar to those created by expectations of a sweeping downward trend. It is true, under floating exchanges the rates tend to move them to a level at which they would eventually cease to make it appear necessary to cover or to hedge and at which they would cease to attract speculators. The process, however, might take days and even weeks, during the course of which the demand for forward exchange facilities would increase under the influence of virtually unlimited risk or of profit prospects. In any case it is very much a matter of opinion at what rate it would be no longer necessary to cover.

Needless to say, scarcity of forward exchange facilities would only arise during periods of sharp fluctuations. The fact that it did not arise in Canada while the dollar was floating must not convey a false feeling of security. Never during its period of floating did the Canadian dollar experience self-aggravating depreciations, because it was always assumed that it would not be allowed to deviate too far from the U.S. dollar. Moreover, the Canadian authorities systematically intervened in the foreign exchange market, bridging gaps between supply and demand.

Crises, such as those experienced in November 1967, March and November 1968 and three times in 1969, would become much more frequent under floating exchanges. The crisis of August 1969 was due to widespread anticipation of a franc devaluation by 15 per cent or less, and the chances of profit or losses were never higher than 15 per cent. Under floating exchanges chances of speculative profit in circumstances similar to those which gave rise to widespread expectation of a devaluation would amount to near-certainty, and the fall of the franc would be expected to be well in excess of 15 per cent. The volume of speculative selling of francs would be much larger, and so would that of hedging operations and the extent of changes in leads and lags.

Would there in such circumstances be enough forward exchange facilities available for commercial requirements? It would depend not only on the volume of demand for forward exchange facilities, which would undoubtedly increase, but also on the total volume of facilities that banks would be able to provide for their customers to meet the increased demand. This is a subject of the utmost importance, which deserves the serious attention of those who are in the position to influence directly or indirectly the decision whether to adopt floating exchanges.

With an amazing degree of cocksureness that usually indicates scant knowledge, advocates of floating rates seek to minimise the adverse effect that wide and incalculable fluctuations of exchange rates would be liable to produce on trade under floating exchanges. They assume that insurance against the resulting exchange risk would present no problem, because importers and exporters would be able to cover the exchange risk with the aid of forward exchange transactions as a matter of routine.

In mitigation of their omission to go more thoroughly into the subject, it must be admitted that until recently specialists failed to provide them with much guidance. For the extensive and rapidly growing literature on forward exchange deals with its technique and with its theory almost exclusively from the point of view of the causes and effects of changes in forward rates. Until recently very little was published about the potential volume of forward exchange facilities.[1] My article entitled 'The Potential Volume of Forward Exchange Facilities', appearing in the December 1968 issue of the *Banca Nazionale del Lavoro Review*, was the first detailed discussion of the subject. The present chapter is based largely but not exclusively on that material. Before the publication of that article, my own contributions to the study of forward exchange had done considerably less than justice to the importance of this aspect of the subject and had failed to go adequately into its complexities, which call for a more detailed analysis.

It is taken widely for granted that, in the absence of exchange controls affecting the freedom of dealing in forward exchanges, the volume of forward exchange operations available for trade purposes – unlike that of spot exchange operations – has no limits either in theory or in practice. Since spot exchange transactions involve immediate delivery of the exchanges sold and immediate payment for them by the buyer – to be exact, delivery and payment after two clear business days – sales of spot exchanges are necessarily limited by the amount of foreign currency that is available to the seller, plus the amount he is able to borrow, and purchases of spot exchanges are limited by the amount of local currency that is available to the buyer,

[1] Paul Einzig, *A Dynamic Theory of Forward Exchange*, 2nd ed. (London, 1967) pp. 12–13, 19–20, 26, 79, 103, 177, 305–6, 472; *A Textbook on Foreign Exchange*, 2nd ed. (London, 1969) pp. 40, 58–9, 176–8, 202–3, 240; *Foreign Exchange Crises*, 2nd ed. (London, 1970) pp. 55–6, 59, 63, 76; *Leads and Lags* (London, 1968) p. 99. See also H. E. Evitt, *A Manual of Foreign Exchange*, 6th ed. by W. W. Syrett, p. 83.

plus the amount he is able to borrow. No delivery or payment is involved, however, in a forward exchange transaction until the contract matures, and even then either of the two sides is in a position to avoid the delivery or the payment by simply settling the exchange difference or by 'rolling' the commitment forward. This is the reason why the limitations that apply to spot exchange transactions – lack of local currency or of foreign currency – do not apply to forward exchange transactions.

Experience during the middle 'sixties appeared to have confirmed the mistaken impression that 'the sky is the limit' to forward exchange transactions. Unlimited support of forward sterling by the Bank of England during 1964–67 resulted in purchases and sales of non-existent dollars running into thousands of millions. Most of those who had bought dollars in anticipation of a devaluation of sterling had not possessed the sterling to pay for the dollars, and the Bank of England had not possessed the dollars it had sold for forward delivery. When during the days following on the devaluation in November 1967 the buyers were called upon to pay for the dollars which they had bought, the Bank of England was able to deliver the dollars it had sold, thanks to the large new credit it obtained. But buyers of dollars found it difficult to secure the sterling to pay for the dollars. They found themselves in a rather embarrassing situation and had to pay fantastic interest rates when borrowing sterling for a few days in order to be able to carry out their part of the contracts. Since, however, the cost of such borrowing represented a negligible fraction of the profits made by speculators who were short in sterling at the moment of its devaluation, this experience did not deter them, or others similarly placed, from resuming their speculative forward exchange operations against sterling a few months later, as soon as sterling came once more under a cloud – even though they were no longer encouraged to do so by an artificially low discount on forward sterling that was brought about by official intervention before the devaluation.

Even in the absence of any ill-advised encouragement of forward exchange operations by a provision of abnormally cheap facilities, there appears to be in theory no limit to their volume. Spot transactions can be reduced or kept down by the application of general or selective credit restrictions. But, as pointed out above, the conclusion of forward exchange contracts does not require cash at the time of their conclusion, or even at the time when they fall due. For this reason the conventional device of monetary policy, credit squeeze, is incapable of limiting the volume of forward exchange transactions to the extent to which it can limit operations in spot exchanges by preventing the purchase or sale of borrowed currency.

Another conventional device, dear money, does tend to discourage forward selling by making it more costly if it is allowed to produce its normal effects on swap margins. But apart from that, it does not place any actual limits to the volume of forward selling. Indeed whenever a devaluation is considered imminent, high interest rates fail to prevent a spectacular increase of forward selling for very short maturities, because even fantastically high forward rates paid on such occasions for a few days as a result of high interest rates usually represent a negligible fraction of the potential profits. The position would be the same under a system of floating rates whenever a depreciation is expected.

The volume of forward exchange transactions is, however, subject to limitations for reasons outside the confines of conventional monetary policy. Such limitations come under the following headings:

(1) Exchange control measures of various kinds.
(2) Instructions to foreign exchange departments by the head offices of their banks to keep the total of their forward commitments, or their forward commitments in particular currencies, or their dealings with particular countries, within certain limits.
(3) Limits applied by most banks to their forward exchange commitments in relation to most other banks.

(4) Limits applied by most banks to forward exchange commitments maturing on any particular day.

Governments and Parliaments have the power to ban forward exchange transactions altogether. They have the power to suppress the free market in forward exchanges – as they did in Britain during and for some time after the Second World War. Or they can limit forward exchange transactions by banning contracts beyond certain time limits, or in certain currencies, or for certain purposes. They can confine forward exchange operations to transactions by 'authorised dealers' and determine the maximum limit to the covered and uncovered forward exchange commitments of each authorised dealer. This is the system that is in operation in Britain and in many other countries at the time of writing. Banks in the U.K. are not supposed to have foreign currency commitments, whether open or covered by forward exchange transactions, beyond a certain authorised limit.

The limits had been fixed fairly low – moreover they were drastically reduced for many banks in 1966 – and their existence does restrict in theory the volume of forward exchange facilities. In practice there are several loopholes:

(1) The limits are overall limits to *net* commitments, which means that a long position in, say, D. marks can be offset by a short position in, say, French francs.
(2) Although returns declaring the positions and commitments are submitted to the Bank of England every week, and more detailed returns every month, banks were inclined until recently to exceed their limits temporarily between the dates for which they have to make their returns. This practice was, however, firmly discouraged by the Bank of England in May 1969, by calling on the banks to submit a return retrospectively concerning their forward commitments on a previous date. Banks which were caught out by this device have now to submit daily returns.
(3) Even if the returns show excesses over the authorised limits, the Bank of England may be willing to accept

reasonable explanations. But repetition of such irregularities is liable to entail suspension of the authorisation to deal in exchanges, and although there have been no such suspensions in practice, the possibility of such penalty discourages banks from exceeding their limits.

(4) In several important countries, such as the U.S., West Germany and Switzerland, there are no official limitations to forward exchange transactions.

I have not come across any recent instance in which banks had to refuse forward exchange facilities to commercial clients because their commitments had reached the officially fixed limits. I am sure that, should such situations arise, banks would be reasonably safe in exceeding temporarily their limits, relying on the assumption that the authorities would accept their explanation. The limits are fixed not in order to handicap business with commercial clients but in order to keep down the volume of speculation and outward arbitrage.

On the other hand, banks are liable to find themselves in a position in which they are unable to meet their customers' genuine commercial requirements for forward exchange facilities, not because of any official restrictions but because their commitments in the market have reached the limit beyond which managements are not prepared to authorise their foreign exchange department to increase the totals. Or the commitments in relation to individual banks may have reached the limits beyond which banks are not prepared to accept each others' names in inter-bank transactions. Such situations did arise for brief periods during the currency chaos of the early 'thirties. They threatened to arise again during the middle 'sixties, when large-scale forward operations, encouraged by the artificially low discount on forward sterling, exhausted the limits applied to the names of some banks. As a result, in 1965–66 one of the leading London banks had to instruct its foreign exchange department to keep down its forward exchange operations to an unavoidable minimum during the next three months, so as to allow the amount of its outstanding forward exchange commitments to decline as and when the contracts matured. This was deemed necessary because the bank in question had exhausted, or nearly exhausted, its limits with most banks. Again in November 1967 a number of banks are known to have reached their limits.

The possibility that such a situation might recur and might assume such an extent that importers and exporters would find it impossible to obtain from their banks the forward exchange facilities they need, looms large on the horizon as a result of the growing pressure in favour of adopting a system of flexible parities or of floating exchange rates. It is my contention that a removal or relaxation of limits fixed under the Bretton Woods system for the fluctuation of exchange rates would greatly increase commercial and other demand for forward exchange facilities and that, at the same time, it would reduce considerably the maximum of such facilities which banks would be in a position to make available for their customers. My reason for this assumption lies partly in the view I take of the way in which flexible parities or freely fluctuating exchange rates would be liable to affect the attitude of industrialists, merchants, investors, speculators, etc., and partly in the view I take of the way in which banks would seek to safeguard themselves in their market operations against the risk arising from wide and unpredictable changes of parities or fluctuations of exchanges.

Under the system of fixed parities and support points, speculative transactions in the broadest sense of the term are undertaken mostly by people who have doubts about the determination or ability of the Governments concerned to resist pressure in favour of a change in the existing parities. After each change, following upon repeated official declarations that the existing parity would be defended at all costs, confidence in the sanctity of such pledges tends to weaken. Nevertheless, as pointed out earlier, except when currency scares becomes acute and changes of parities are considered imminent, the opinion of bankers and businessmen concerned with foreign exchange transaction is sharply divided on the question whether the Government is able and willing to defend the existing parities. A high proportion of those concerned usually believe that the Government, when disclaiming any intention to devalue, means what it says. Otherwise each currency scare would develop into a landslide such as actually occurred in November 1967 from the moment the British Government, in its wisdom, came to abstain from reaffirming its pledge not to devalue sterling.

Should the system of flexible parities or of floating exchange rates be adopted, it would become the Government's declared policy to abstain from resisting any selling pressure on its exchange. The whole idea of the system of flexible or floating exchanges is to allow the exchange rates to find their own level without trying to defend them. A depreciation or a repetition of devaluations would then continue until the trend is automatically halted or reversed through the unimpeded and unaided forces operating in a market free of official intervention. Until that stage is reached, whenever there is some obvious adverse factor in operation, the near-certainty that the resulting selling pressure would not be resisted would induce most people who have interests to protect to cover or hedge against the exchange movements they expect. It would induce another set of operators to exploit the high degree of possibility for making speculative profits on such unhindered exchange trends. There would be, therefore, a considerable increase in the demand for forward exchange facilities both for speculative and non-speculative purposes. The knowledge that the authorities would be 'neutral' in face of the adverse trend would greatly stimulate such demand.

The banks' ability to meet such an increased demand would be far from unlimited. It is true, during the various periods of currency chaos between the wars there were most of the time no difficulties in obtaining forward exchange facilities, providde that the customers were creditworthy. Even if their creditworthiness was doubted, banks were able to secure themselves against the risk of default by insisting on receiving from their customers a deposit that they deemed sufficient to cover any likely losses arising from exchange movements.

Since pre-war days the situation has changed, however, partly as a result of the spectacular increase in the volume and value of foreign trade, and partly because importers and exporters have become much more foreign-exchange conscious. The practice of inventory hedging – the covering of the risk of a fall in the price of imported goods as a result of a devaluation of the exporting country's currency – has become incomparably more prevalent in a number of countries (not in Britain, where it is not permitted) and is applied to an increasing extent. There has been a spectacular increase in international investment and in the volume of investment-hedging – the covering of the risk of a depreciation of the foreign investment in terms of the investor's currency as a result of a devaluation of the currency of the country in which he holds a portfolio investment or a direct investment. This again is forbidden in Britain. While non-residents usually aggravate pressures on sterling by hedging against their British investments, U.K. residents are, oddly enough, forbidden to support sterling by hedging against their foreign investments. In addition, the expansion of the Euro-currency market and of the Euro-bond market has created a considerable demand for forward exchange facilities.

Admittedly, pure speculation has declined, but in times of acute crises – such as we witnessed during the flight from the pound in November 1967 – it is apt to exceed considerably its pre-war extent. So the fact that the banks were able to meet their customers' requirements of forward exchange facilities most of the time in the inter-war period when exchange rates were fluctuating or were subject to frequent changes of parities should not lead us into a false feeling of security about their ability to meet the requirements if the world should relapse into currency chaos as a result of more frequent changes of parities or of the adoption of floating exchanges.

What would make the banks' task to satisfy their customers' requirements even more difficult is that, simultaneously with the increase in the demand for forward exchange facilities, there would be a sharp decline in the maximum of such facilities that the banks would be able to offer their customers. This decline would be due to the desire of bank managements to play for safety by reducing the limits for their total open positions and even for their covered commitments, for their open and covered positions in particular currencies or countries, and for the names of individual banks. Increased risks of heavy losses through unforeseen exchange movements or through new exchange-control measures might tend to induce managements to err on the conservative side and impose unreasonably low limits on their foreign exchange departments. At present most foreign exchange departments are treated fairly liberally by their head offices so long as they are able to show favourable results. But their managements might become inclined to interfere with their freedom if they had a run of bad luck. The removal of the IMF limits to the fluctuations of spot rates, under which profit possibilities as well as risks are limited in existing circumstances – barring changes in parities – would increase the incalculable risk of substantial losses. The natural reaction of managements would be to reduce the existing limits.

The practice of insisting on deposits by customers on their forward exchange transactions, which has declined considerably, might be resumed. What would be infinitely worse for customers, the extent to which their banks would be able to satisfy their requirements might become reduced, because the banks might have to 'ration' their reduced volume of forward exchange facilities, owing to the contraction in the volume of total forward exchange facilities at their disposal in the market. If their forward commitments even approach the limits to which other banks are prepared to take their names for such commitments, they might find it difficult to undo in the market their new forward commitments in relation to their customers.

This brings us to the examination of the most difficult and least explored aspect of our subject – the practice of most banks of limiting their forward exchange commitments in relation to most other banks, and the broader implications of this practice. The main difficulty of discussing this subject arises from the secrecy which surrounds the practice, and from the almost infinite variety of its application by various banks.

There are other limits for names of banks in inter-bank dealings, besides the limits on forward exchange commitments. Indeed the practice of applying maximum limits to transactions in Euro-currencies or inter-bank sterling loans is a great deal stricter than the limits to forward exchange commitments, because the degree of risk is higher. If a bank defaults on a forward exchange contract – whether through insolvency or in consequence of exchange restrictions – the resulting loss does not exceed the exchange rate difference, which in any case need not necessarily be adverse. But Euro-currency or inter-bank sterling transactions are unsecured loans and default might mean total loss of the entire amounts involved. Hence the practice under which foreign exchange brokers are willing to disclose the name of the would-be borrower of Euro-currency deposits to the would-be lender before the deal is concluded. The limits for names are much lower for such transactions than for forward exchange transactions.

Many banks also have another kind of limit for names – the total limit of spot and forward commitments maturing on the same day. They seek to safeguard themselves against the 'delivery risk' arising from the impossibility of synchronising absolutely the delivery of foreign currencies and the payment for them in national currency. Although they must take place on the same day, there is apt to be a discrepancy of several hours, and there is a remote possibility that a bank, having made the payment in accordance with the contract, does not receive the foreign currencies it had bought for spot delivery in two days or for forward delivery. Hence the desire of many banks to limit the total amount receivable from the same bank on the same day. This practice need not necessarily limit the total of forward exchange facilities, because it does not affect commitments maturing on different dates. For our present purposes the practice of banks of applying limits for the *total* forward exchange commitments of every other bank is what really matters.

As I pointed out above, the way in which banks apply this practice varies widely. Very broadly speaking, there is a marked difference between what we may conveniently call the American practice and the British practice. Banks in the United States apply their limits to the *gross* outstanding commitments in their relation with other banks, while British banks in general apply it to the *net* difference between their long and short positions in their relations with other banks. The reason why American banks follow a much more stringent rule lies in American bankruptcy law under which default by a bank does not exempt the bank which is the victim of that default from honouring its own obligation in relation to the defaulter. That being so, American banks are not satisfied with merely limiting the net difference between their purchases of foreign exchanges from, and sales of foreign exchange to, any one bank. They feel impelled to limit even the gross total of their commitments in relation to any one bank. This practice is so firmly established that it is pursued even by American bank branches abroad, although they operate under the laws of the country of their residence.

In Britain itself the practice of fixing limits for names varies widely among banks. Some banks are much more liberal than others, and have virtually no limits for banks of their own class, whether in London or abroad. They have very vague and elastic limits for smaller banks of good standing, and the decision is left to the head of their foreign exchange department. Other banks observe very strict limits for all names. Their attitude gave rise to some difficulties between 1964 and 1967, whenever they were supporting forward sterling on behalf of the Bank of England on a large scale. Owing to the large amounts involved, their limits for banks to which they were selling forward dollars was actually reached in a number of instances. The banks for whose names the limit was reached, being unable to buy forward dollars at the official rates from other banks in the market because all banks other than those operating for the Bank of England were buyers, had to buy through some other bank whose commitments in relation to the bank in charge of 'control' operations had not reached their limit. Such use of the names of other banks cost them something like ⅛ per cent to ¼ per cent in the rate.

What matters from the point of view with which we are here concerned is that there is a distinct possibility that all or most banks might reach their limits in relation to each other. Such a situation might well have arisen in a big way if, instead of devaluing on 17 November 1967, the Government had sought to hold sterling at $2.78 a little longer. Banks might have ceased to be in a position to undo in the market their commitments undertaken in relation to their customers and might have had to refuse additional forward exchange facilities to them.

The practice of limits for names is a nightmare for foreign exchange brokers. While they are generally aware of the unwillingness of certain banks to take certain names for forward exchange transactions, they have no means of knowing if and when the limits for forward exchange transactions with banks whose names are usually taken have been reached. Even if a name has been refused on the ground that the limit has been reached, transactions through other channels might reduce the net amount of the commitments between the two banks, so that a few minutes after a refusal the bank concerned might become once more willing to take the name in question.

One of the absolute rules that govern banker–broker relationships is that in foreign exchange transactions – as distinct from Euro-currency transactions – the two parties must not be informed about the name of the bank which provides the counterpart until the deal is definitely concluded. If a bank, on learning the name of the other bank, tells the broker that it cannot accept that bank's name because its limit for that name has been exhausted, the broker is placed in a very awkward position. In no circumstances must he inform the bank in question that its name has been refused on the ground that its limit has been reached. One of the main justifications for dealing through brokers is precisely that a bank need not disclose to another bank – which might well be of first-class standing – its unwillingness to take the latter name. Such refusals are among the most closely-guarded secrets of the brokers.

If a name is unexpectedly refused after the finalisation of the deal, there are various formulas with the aid of which the broker may try to cancel the transaction, mostly through pleading misunderstanding. Frequent recurrence of such cancellations are detrimental to the broker's goodwill with the bank concerned, even though he is in no way to blame. So in many instances he looks round frantically in the market to provide an alternative counterpart, on identical terms. It might even settle the exchange difference if the counterpart can only be secured on less favourable terms, under arrangements made through the intermediary of the Foreign Exchange and Deposit Brokers Association.

Having dealt with the technical aspects of the practice of fixing limits for names, our next step is to examine its broader aspects. In order to be able to do so effectively it would be of the utmost importance to be in a position to ascertain the grand total of the amounts to which banks are prepared to take each other's names for forward exchange transactions. It would give us an idea of the potential maximum of forward exchange facilities and of changes in the amount of the potential maximum. Unfortunately, owing to the secrecy which surrounds the practice, and even more owing to its different application by various banks and to the flexibility of its rules of application even by the same bank, this is quite impossible. We have to be content with registering the fact that in given circumstances the practice is liable to limit the grand total of forward exchange transactions in the market, and therefore also the forward exchange facilities which banks are in a position to offer their customers. Even though some banks profess to have virtually no limits for good names, if the limits applied by the majority of banks should divert too many transactions to them, a stage is bound to be reached at which they too would apply limits and would themselves become subject to limits.

I must plead guilty of gross oversimplification in my previous writings on the subject of limits for names. For instance, in my *Leads and Lags* I stated 'the sum total of these limits constitutes in theory the maximum limit of forward exchange facilities which the banks are able to offer to their commercial clients'. This principle, to the extent to which it is correct, is of considerable importance from the point of view of both foreign exchange theory and foreign exchange policy. It gave me much satisfaction, when I enunciated it, to feel that I was the first to enunciate it. For this reason, among others, it is with the utmost regret and reluctance that I now feel impelled to admit that, after careful reconsideration, I have come to realise the gross inadequacy of the formula. Even though the basic principle that the volume of forward exchange facilities available to trade is liable to be affected by limits to names is incontestable, the form in which I had stated it is inaccurate and misleading.

For one thing, the formula according to which the aggregate of limits to names represents the maximum of forward exchange facilities is grossly oversimplified. I have always distrusted any economic theory which, in accordance with the all-too-prevailing fashion, seeks to fit economic theories, situations or changes into the strait-jacket of some mathematical or arithmetical formula. To my mind some econometricians are inclined at times to indulge in wishful thinking by adjusting their theories, and even the factual material on which their theories are based, in such a way as to make them conform to figures which they put forward with a higher degree of assurance than could possibly be justified on the basis of a more penetrating analysis of the highly involved subjects concerned.

My fundamental distrust of fallacious econometric arguments in economics expressed in terms of simple arithmetic makes it all the more difficult for me to find an acceptable excuse for having committed the very same offence which I often criticised when committed by others. There is nothing for it but to admit candidly that my formula is mistaken in more than one respect. In some respect it overrates the maximum volume of forward exchange facilities that is determined by the total of limits, while in another respect it underrates that maximum. The practical effects of its distortions tend therefore to offset each other to a high degree. But I have no means of estimating, let alone ascertaining, the extent to which my revised and amplified theory calls for a modification – if any – of the conclusion based on my original over-simplified theory, or even to form a very definite opinion about the direction in which it has to be modified on balance.

(1) The formula that the maximum of forward exchange facilities available to banks' customers is equal to the total of the limits to which banks are prepared to take each others' names for forward exchange transactions is incorrect even from the point of view of its simple arithmetic.

(2) In any case, it assumes a uniform practice and disregards the effect of divergences between the practical application of limits for names.

(3) It also overlooks the extent to which banks are in a position to 'marry' their buying and selling transactions with their customers.

(4) It overlooks the extent to which forward exchange transactions of banks with their customers are, or can be, covered by spot transactions leading to changes in the banks' assets or liabilities in terms of foreign currencies.

(5) It overlooks the obvious fact that banks cannot reserve for their commercial customers all forward exchange facilities that they are able to cover in the market.

(6) On the other hand, it also overlooks the extent to which a reduction in the amount of forward exchange commitments of a non-commercial origin can increase the amount of facilities available for commercial customers.

My original formula overlooks the obvious fact that the same transaction in the foreign exchange market is apt to increase or reduce the commitments of *both* parties in relation to each other, so that it is apt to change the grand total of unavailed limits by *twice* the amount involved.

Let us assume that bank A's limit for bank B is $200 million while bank B's limit for bank A is also $200 million, and that up to a given date bank A had sold to bank B $50 million for forward delivery while it had bought from bank B $40 million for forward delivery. Under the American system the unused limit of both banks in relation to each other is reduced by $50 million, making a total reduction of $100 million in the forward exchange facilities they are able to offer to their customers. Under the British system the limit is only reduced by twice the difference of $10 million between forward purchases and sales, that is, by a total of $20 million. What matters from the point of view with which we are here concerned is that under both systems the total of the unused limits is reduced not merely by the gross or net amount of the outstanding commitments but by *twice* their amount, since each bank deducts the amount in question from the unused amount of its limit. The maximum of forward exchange facilities which *each* bank is able to offer its customers is reduced by the amount of the transactions with the other bank.

Conversely, if as a result of a forward exchange transaction the *net* forward commitments of the banks in question are reduced, the total of their unavailed limits is increased by twice the amount of the transaction under the British system. Buying and selling transactions are liable to offset each other to a large extent, so that the net outstanding balance tends to be relatively small. Under the American system, on the other hand, the gross outstanding commitments tend to increase with such transaction and the limits are liable to be reached much earlier. The unavailed amounts are not reduced by a transaction in the opposite sense but are increased further. Owing to the growing importance of American banks in the foreign exchange market, the exhaustion of their limits for other banks is liable to make forward dealing in dollars increasingly difficult during a prolonged period of pressure.

If American banks exhaust their limits for each other and for non-American banks before the latter exhaust their limits for each other or for American banks, difficulties are liable to arise in undoing forward dollar commitments. This would not necessarily mean that dealings in forward dollars would come to a halt in European markets, but if American banks are unable to provide counterparts for them, European banks exhaust each others' limits, even though they are only concerned with net commitments. The fact that each transaction is apt to reduce the total limits available for *all* banks not by its amount but by twice its amount must be borne in mind.

To the extent to which banks are in a position to 'marry' their buying and selling orders from their customers without having to undo their commitments in the market, their capacity to provide their customers with forward exchange facilities exceeds the limits to which other banks take their names. Even if it is not always easy to match a buying order with a selling order for the same date, discrepancies between maturity dates can usually be offset by time arbitrage operations in the market, which would not affect the total of available limits under the British system, though it would affect that total under the American system. But it must be borne in mind that during periods of one-sided pressure on a currency most commercial operations, as indeed most other operations, tend to be in the same sense. When, rightly or wrongly, a devaluation of the national currency is expected, most of any bank's customers are buyers of foreign currencies. The extent to which it is possible to 'marry' customers' buying and selling orders is apt to decline to vanishing point just at a time when market facilities for covering are liable to become exhausted through the operation of the limits applied to names.

Banks whose name has reached its limit for forward exchange operations can still operate in spot exchanges. The possibilities of covering a forward exchange transaction with a customer by a spot transaction in the market are, therefore, liable to increase the maximum limit of forward exchange facilities available for customers. It is of course a well-established practice of banks to cover forward outright transactions – whether with customers or with other banks – by spot transactions in the first instance and to undo the resulting covered commitment by means of a swap transaction in the market, which restores the *status quo* that existed prior to the forward outright transaction. But for various reasons banks might prefer, instead of restoring the *status quo*, to accept the changed situation by allowing the covering spot transaction to reduce or increase their foreign currency holdings or to reduce or increase their foreign currency liabilities. They might want to link up the covering of their open positions with passive interest arbitrage subject to the official limits.

My original formula failed to allow for non-commercial forward exchange requirements which banks also have to meet, in addition to meeting the requirements of their commercial customers. Even if banks discriminate against obviously speculative requirements, such discrimination is only practicable in respect of their transactions with their customers outside the market. In inter-bank transactions – whether within the same markets or with banks abroad – banks have no means of knowing whether the forward exchange transactions serve commercial or speculative purposes. In order to be 'in the market', banks have to deal frequently with other banks. In addition, they have to provide facilities for genuine investment-hedging by non-residents, for covering exchange risk on future interest or dividend receipts or payments and on future capital repayments, etc. They may want to operate also on their own account, to increase or reduce their open positions. All these requirements tend to reduce the forward exchange facilities available for the commercial requirements of their customers, unless the latter are given absolute priority.

Finally, my formula did not allow for the possibility of a drastic reduction of a bank's forward exchange commitments of a non-commercial origin, whether under official pressure or under pressure by commercial customers, or by policy decision at the head office. It is estimated that in normal conditions the turnover in the market is several times larger than the banks' turnover with their commercial customers. There is ample scope for a reduction of the former for the benefit of the latter if the limits to which the bank's name is taken are reached or approached. Earlier in this chapter we quoted an actual instance in which this was done.

To sum up, reservations under (1) and (5) qualifying the theory that the volume of forward exchange facilities available for trade purposes depends on the grand total of limits for names in interbank dealings tend to reduce the theoretical maximum of forward exchange facilities below the amount suggested by my original formula. On the other hand, the reservations under (3), (4) and (6) tend to increase that maximum. Reservation under (2) simply increases the degree of uncertainty about the whereabouts of the maximum. It is impossible to form a dependable opinion about the net effect of all these conflicting reservations.

What matters is that, even allowing for all reservations, a maximum limit set by the grand total of limits for names in the market does exist somewhere, although its whereabouts are impossible to ascertain even in theory, let alone in practice. Its existence is far from being generally realised. It must be taken into consideration by the authorities before deciding to embark on policies which are liable to increase commercial or other requirements of forward exchange facilities, or which are liable to cause a reduction of limits for names.

The above consideration constitutes a powerful argument against the adoption of flexible exchanges with frequent changes of parities, or of floating exchanges with no parities at all. Under either system the limits would be reduced. In the absence of official intervention to maintain forward margins at an artificial level, the change in supply–demand relationship of forward exchange facilities might raise the cost of covering or hedging to a prohibitive level, or it might even deprive legitimate interests altogether of the facilities they require. In such circumstances, many importers and exporters might prefer to forgo the transaction rather than risk losses through uncovered exchange movements, and many foreign investors might prefer to repatriate their capital. I need not dwell on the possible consequences of such decisions by a large number of firms or investors.

Of course the authorities are always in a position to provide additional forward exchange facilities for approved purposes. Moreover, as far as exporters are concerned, in Britain and in some other countries there is actually a system of official insurance of exchange risk in operation. During the war and for some time after, the Bank of England provided forward exchange facilities for importers as well as for exporters. But under such arrangements the Government would assume the full exchange risk on foreign trade instead of leaving this function to the banks and to the foreign exchange market. This would deprive the Government of one of the main advantages of the system of flexible or floating rates compared with fixed parities under which the authorities have to support the national currency at a certain spot rate. A Central Banker once told me that whenever a Central Bank holds the rate at an artificial level, it attracts an amazing volume of one-sided pressure from every part of the globe. As past experience has shown, official forward exchange facilities are also apt to be exploited by using them unilaterally, in accordance with the prevailing trend. This was what happened in 1949. It was the one-sided use of official facilities resulting from the lengthening of leads and lags that threatened to deplete the official reserves and forced Sir Stafford Cripps to break his oft-repeated promise not to devalue sterling.

Moreover, discriminating official allocation of forward exchange facilities for the benefit of commercial transactions by residents does not meet the requirements of non-residents, whether traders or speculators. Their operations would result in a depreciation of the forward exchange concerned in foreign markets.

The emergence of a two-tier system under which different

rates would operate for officially approved commercial transactions and for other transactions would produce a strongly adverse world-wide psychological effect highly detrimental to sterling. The unofficial rate would be widely regarded as the barometer indicating the true value of sterling, so that its depreciation would induce U.K. importers and exporters to take full advantage of the favourable official rates by lengthening their leads and lags. Considering that the average lengthening of leads and lags by a single week would mean loss of reserves at the rate of £240 million per annum, the case against such a two-tier system is unanswerable, as far as a major currency such as sterling is concerned. Unless forward covering and hedging facilities are available at reasonable cost for all genuine commercial transactions, a decline in the volume of foreign trade might result in a world-wide slump, with incalculable financial, economic, social and political consequences.

The fact that during the long period of floating exchanges between the wars the dangerous situation envisaged in this chapter only arose on rare occasions and for relatively brief periods does not justify us in ignoring or underrating the possibility of its more frequent recurrence in case of an adoption of floating exchanges in the totally different situation prevailing at present. As I remarked above, requirements for forward exchange facilities have increased very considerably. Importers and exporters have become much more forward-exchange-minded. The volume of foreign trade has greatly expanded. The volume of non-commercial transactions too has greatly expanded especially, those arising from international capital movements.

The development of the Euro-currency markets alone has added potential buying or selling of foreign exchanges amounting to tens of billions of dollars. The fact that in 1967 many Sterling Area countries did not devalue in sympathy with sterling and the losses suffered in consequence as a result of uncovered commitments resulted in a considerable increase in the demand for forward exchange facilities even between countries within the Sterling Area. Today the potential demand for forward exchange facilities is a multiple of its pre-war amount. The problems arising from it should not be dismissed lightly. While theoretical economists may wish to ignore them out of existence even after their attention was drawn to this aspect of the subject, Central Bankers and Treasury officials could ill afford to embark on experiments with floating rates that are liable to fluctuate widely without allowing for the broader implications of this technical point.

CHAPTER FOURTEEN

Floating Rates between Currency Areas

As already pointed out earlier, most advocates of floating exchanges are vague on the vitally important question as to whether they wish the system to operate exclusively in their own country, or in a limited number of select countries, or in all countries. Some of them do envisage, however, a situation in which a number of countries would become grouped into two or more currency areas. Within each area parities or exchange rates would be fixed, while between the areas, and also in relation to 'independent currencies', exchange rates would float freely. What might happen is that two or more principal currencies would fluctuate in terms of each other, and a number of minor currencies would become the satellites of the major currencies, maintaining stable relationships with one or the other of them. Alternatively, a number of currencies would be kept stable in terms of gold and therefore in terms of each other, while the rest of the currencies would fluctuate in terms of the stable currencies. Possibly some of the floating currencies would be kept stable in terms of each other.

Many of the arguments against the system of floating exchanges apply whether these exchanges float between individual currencies or between currency areas. But the disadvantages from floating exchanges are mitigated by the maintenance of stability within the currency areas. The advantages of fixed exchanges from the point of view of foreign trade, international capital movement and business planning are of the same character whether stability is confined to a currency area or to a much larger sphere, even though the benefits apply to a much narrower sphere if stability is confined to a currency area only.

But in order that stability within a currency area should produce its full beneficial effects, it would be necessary for that currency area to be much more than some form of economic union involving stable exchange rates and a customs union with differential tariffs against imports from non-member countries. The member countries would have to subordinate to a high degree their sovereignty to some central authority empowered to ensure a high degree of uniformity of monetary, fiscal and economic policies. Otherwise disequilibrium would inevitably develop sooner or later between the currencies of member countries. Their fixed parities would no longer correspond to their trade equilibrium level. Balance of payments deficits and surpluses between them could assume such abnormal proportions as to disrupt the currency area.

Such a state of affairs is not likely to develop in a currency area that includes both highly advanced and underdeveloped countries, because in their relationship it is natural that the former should become creditors of the latter. For the sake of the advantages derived from stability of their exchanges, it might be worth their while to put up with the disadvantages of disequilibrium. But then the same may be said to be true about stability of exchanges in relation to countries outside the currency areas.

Advocates of floating exchanges who admit that there is much to be said about fixed exchanges between member countries of currency areas are guilty of inconsistency. Surely if stability is worth having within a limited number of countries, it is surely even more worth having within a larger number of countries. If arguments in favour of stability within currency areas are valid, the case for extending the sphere of their stability as far as possible is unanswerable.

Of course the system of stability within currency areas and fluctuations of exchanges between currency areas need not be created by deliberate action. It might develop spontaneously because a number of Governments deem it expedient to maintain their currencies stable in relation to one or the other of the major currencies, allowing them to fluctuate in relation to the other currencies in sympathy with the movements of the major currency concerned. As a result the leading currency of the area comes to enjoy the benefit of stability that exists under fixed parities, even though to a limited extent only. The same is true about the countries which choose to become members of such informal currency areas.

But floating exchanges between currency areas have the same disadvantages as floating exchanges between individual countries. Movements between them and stable exchanges, or between them and other floating exchanges, are liable to become self-aggravating. The 'ratchet' effect, under which a recovery that follows a depreciation is followed by another depreciation which goes further than the previous one, would operate between exchanges of currency areas. Banks might be unable to meet their clients' forward exchange requirements.

A competitive depreciation race is liable to develop between currency areas in the same way as it is liable to develop between individual countries with floating exchanges. This actually happened in 1933–34, when there was a competitive depreciation race between the Sterling Area and the group of currencies which were kept stable in relation to the dollar, even if there was no formal arrangement between the latter and the dollar.

International trade would be handicapped during periods of acute crises by lack of forward exchange facilities in the same way as under pure floating exchanges. Admittedly, demand for facilities for trade within the areas would be limited. But instability in relation to currencies outside currency areas would be liable to undermine confidence even in stability within the currency areas. This is an important point which deserves closer examination.

Countries in the same currency areas are liable to be affected to a different degree by identical fluctuations of their exchanges in relation to exchanges outside the currency area. For instance, if the Common Market were a currency area, an appreciation of the fixed exchange rates of its members in relation to the dollar, sterling and other currencies would affect the German economy and the French economy to a different degree, among other reasons because the balance of power between trade unions and employers is different in the two countries. The German economy might be in a better position to overcome the effects of an appreciation than the French economy. Disequilibrium would develop between the economies of the two countries. Since the exchange rate between them would remain fixed, their disequilibrium would lead to a German trade surplus and a French trade deficit on Franco-German trade.

In a similar way if a currency area should allow its exchange rate to depreciate in terms of exchange rates of the other currency areas or of individual countries outside the currency area, the degree of the resulting inflation would differ in individual member countries according to the degree of discipline in the economy. The German economy might be in a better position to keep down the extent of the inflation than the French economy. The resulting disequilibrium would again mean an increased French deficit on Franco-German trade. Should such a deficit assume considerable dimensions, it might lead to a disintegration of the currency union.

In any case, as a result of recent experience, the idea of currency unions is now at a discount. After the Franco-German conflict of views during 1968–69 on the revaluation of the D. mark and the devaluation of the franc, it is doubtful if the Common Market would ever become a currency area in the real sense of the term. The disintegration of the Sterling Area which has been proceeding under our very eyes is in itself sufficient to discourage the establishment of new formal currency areas. Nor is the Franc Area certain to survive more grave domestic political and economic troubles in France and their effects on the French economy. Any system based on stability within currency areas and instability in relation to currencies outside the currency areas could have no dependable foundations so long as independent monetary and economic policies are pursued within member countries, and so long as the various nations react differently to identical policy measures.

It is conceivable, nevertheless, that a number of Western European currencies would retain their present stability in relation to gold and that they would remain stable in relation to each other, while a number of other countries would adopt a system of floating exchanges. A similar situation did actually arise during the 'thirties when a number of countries formed the 'gold bloc', while others like Britain and, for a short time, the United States, adopted floating exchanges. A number of currencies were kept stable in relation to sterling or the dollar without a formal arrangement to that effect.

Although the currency of each 'gold bloc' country was affected by the view taken in the market about the possibility that the country concerned might abandon the 'gold bloc', by and large gold currencies fluctuated in sympathy with each other in terms of floating currencies. Such a state of affairs is apt to be purely temporary, as is shown by the experience of the 'gold bloc' in the thirties. As a result of the adverse pressure on stable currencies caused by the depreciation and undervaluation of the floating exchanges, the 'gold bloc' abandoned the defence of its parities in 1936 and its members devalued. Subsequently some of them adopted a flexible exchange.

The operation of currency areas would not save the world from currency chaos and a competitive depreciation race or devaluation race. Any changes in the exchange rate of one major country is liable to alter the equilibrium rates for all countries, albeit to a varying degree. For instance, as a result of a depreciation of sterling the exports and imports of individual countries in a currency area would be affected to a different degree. To restore the balance between their imports and exports it might therefore become necessary to adjust their exchanges in relation to each other. Pressure to discontinue rigidity of exchange rates within currency areas might then become difficult to resist.

However, notwithstanding the above arguments, if the

choice were between a system of universal floating exchanges or of exchanges between currency areas, it would be decidedly preferable to have a system under which there is stability at least within groups of countries, even though the maintenance of that stability would be made more difficult by fluctuations of other currencies.

Of course if the contention of advocates of floating exchanges about the advantages of their system were valid, then it would be preferable from the point of view of each country if their currency, and their currency alone, would float, while all other currencies would maintain their fixed parities in relation to gold and in relation to each other. But the adoption of floating exchanges is liable to be infectious – not because of any advantages but because it is tempting to take the line of least resistance and because a depreciation of a major currency would affect all exchanges – and it would not be confined to one country for very long. It is of course conceivable that currencies of certain countries which have close financial and trade relations with each other would fluctuate in sympathy with each other even in the absence of any deliberate policies to that end. But the existence of currency areas, whether formal or informal, would not prevent the development of currency chaos, even if its extent might be somewhat mitigated by the existence of limited areas of stability – unless and until those areas get out of equilibrium in relation to important floating currencies.

CHAPTER FIFTEEN

Instability Tempered by Intervention

EXTREME supporters of the system of floating exchanges are firmly opposed to any official intervention in the foreign exchange market to influence their movements. This is because they are convinced that it is only if exchanges are left severely alone that they could automatically adapt themselves to their equilibrium level. In reality, in the absence of official intervention, exchange rates would be completely exposed to the caprices of any trend, speculative or otherwise, whether equilibrating or disequilibrating in its effects.

Opponents of the gold standard had argued against it mainly on the ground that under that system the world's economy is at the mercy of the caprices of nature, because of the fluctuations of gold output, depending as it largely does on fortuitous discoveries of new gold deposits and on the incidence of the exhaustion of the existing gold deposits. But if the choice is between the caprices of nature and the caprices of 'gnomes', the former would be preferable, especially since it is now possible to supplement the international gold reserves by additional international monetary resources through the operation of the gold exchange standard, IMF drawing rights and other arrangements or institutions.

Opponents of the Bretton Woods system of fixed parities argue against that system mainly on the ground that whenever the 'gnomes' choose to attack a currency, the Government of the country concerned has to apply unpleasant economic measures in its defence. What they refuse to realise is that under floating exchanges without official intervention the power of the 'gnomes' would be infinitely stronger. Exchange rates, which determine prices, interest rates, employment, etc., would be influenced very extensively by speculative movements instead of being determined either by the caprices of nature or by policies of responsible Governments. Under floating rates the 'gnomes' would determine domestic and international economic trends through their influence on exchange rates. It is, therefore, no exaggeration to call the system of floating exchanges without intervention 'gnomocracy'. Governments would simply abdicate their power, and would relinquish their responsibility, over value of the national currency. That task would be left to the mercy of speculation.

Many extreme supporters of floating exchanges who are opposed to intervention in the foreign exchange market concede that influencing floating exchanges by means of conventional monetary policy devices might be permissible. Professor Machlup provides one of the exceptions. 'The introduction of freely flexible exchange rates', he states in his *Plans for Reform of the International Monetary System*, 'would relieve the Central Banks once for all of any functions in the international payments system and would remove any requirement to hold reserves for foreign payments.' He seriously believes that the monetary authorities could safely leave the task of determining exchange rates to speculators and other private interests concerned with foreign exchanges, because 'equality of receipts and disbursements would be secured through the free adjustment of foreign exchange rates to the supply-and-demand structure of the moment'. But if there is one thing that is certain, it is that the rate at which receipts and disbursement would be equal would not be identical with trade equilibrium rate.

As a result of the increased power of speculators under his system, and in the complete absence of official support of the exchange, the application of conventional drastic monetary devices might become imperative. Such devices would have to be applied in even larger doses than under fixed exchanges if the authorities should want to save the national currency from drifting into runaway inflation as a result of its unrestrained self-aggravating downward trend. In the past in most instances Governments did intervene during periods of fluctuating exchanges, to regulate or moderate the fluctuations not only by means of conventional monetary devices but also by means of direct operations in the foreign exchange market. The scope of such intervention varied.

During the 'thirties the purpose of some Governments was to prevent 'imported deflation' by causing a depreciation of the exchange rather than allow a depreciation and undervaluation of foreign currencies to depress domestic prices and increase unemployment. In other instances Government intervention pursued merely tactical ends, such as a bear squeeze. The officially declared aim of the British authorities in the early 'thirties was to 'iron out fluctuations' without trying to interfere with basic trends. This was also the object of intervention by the Canadian authorities in the 'fifties when they sought to regulate the tendencies of the Canadian dollar during its floating period, largely by means of intervention in the foreign exchange market.

Under floating exchanges, as under fixed exchanges, intervention may aim at preventing or moderating an unwanted appreciation or depreciation, or at accentuating a movement which suited their purpose. For instance, during the brief period of the floating D. mark the Bundesbank intervened to step up the appreciation of its currency, so as to prepare the way for its revaluation.

Intervention may assume the passive form of maintaining a peg – a temporary rate at which the authorities are prepared to satisfy private demand for foreign exchange, or, as the case may be, to buy up excess supply of foreign exchanges, in the market. But they can move the peg frequently, if necessary several times a day. Alternatively, the authorities may intervene from time to time to mitigate an exchange movement without attempting to hold the rates at any particular level. Intervention may also assume the form of supplying importers and other approved classes of buyers with the foreign exchanges they require. Or it may assume the form of diverting from the market certain large transactions which would otherwise trigger off an unwanted movement on the rates.

Active intervention means that the authorities take the initiative for engaging in foreign exchange operations for the purpose of influencing the exchange rate. Such intervention can be effected in spot exchanges or in forward exchanges or in both.

Under the gold standard intervention was purely passive. It consisted of buying and selling gold at fixed prices whenever exchange movements tended to go beyond gold points. It was for arbitrageurs to take the initiative for engaging in gold shipments whenever exchange movements made this profitable. Under the letter of the IMF rules, the task of member countries (other than the United States) is confined to buying or selling dollars to prevent exchange rates from rising or falling beyond official support points. But on many occasions the authorities intervene before the rates reach their support points, to prevent the rates from rising or falling to the figures at which it becomes their duty to intervene.

In order to be able to intervene in spot exchanges, the authorities have to possess or borrow substantial resources of foreign exchanges. This is one of the reasons why some advocates of floating exchanges are opposed to intervention. Machlup and others argue in favour of floating exchanges partly on the ground that it would remove the necessity for keeping large reserves. It is of course possible to support the exchange by operating in forward rates without having to possess large reserves. This probably explains why some advocates of floating rates are in favour of intervention in forward exchanges – or were in its favour until that device came to be discredited by the disastrous result of its misuse for unlimited support of sterling during 1964–67.

Inflationists want to adopt the system of floating exchanges because under it authorities need never worry about the decline of their reserves. They could then inflate to their heart's desire, because it would not be necessary for the authorities to acquire and maintain reserves for the sake of preventing domestic inflation from producing its normal effect on the exchanges.

To be able to intervene successfully, the authorities would have to possess even larger reserves under floating exchanges than under fixed exchanges, owing to the demoralising effect of wide exchange movements. Unless the Government had an impressive reserve, it could not make itself felt in the market. The absence of a large reserve would encourage speculators to attack the defenceless exchanges. The Government would not be in a position to engage in bear squeezes unless and until a speculative movement became obviously overdone. The reason why larger reserves would be required than under fixed parities is that rates at which the authorities would have to choose to support the exchange would not inspire the same degree of confidence as gold parities or official support points. In accordance with the official policy, such temporary rates would be liable to be changed at any moment.

Only an ever-present possibility of effective intervention thanks to the possession of formidable reserves would tend to discourage speculators from operating on a large scale in a sense inconvenient to the Government.

Needless to say, excessive upward or downward movements of exchanges are liable to become reversed sooner or later even in the absence of intervention, when the market itself comes to realise that an exchange movement is overdone. But intervention would prevent an unbalancing self-aggravating movement from going as far as it would go in the absence of intervention. It could also exaggerate the recovery which would come as a reaction after the depreciation has passed its climax, and it could enable the authorities to make substantial profits through bear squeezes.

The existence of substantial reserves for the purpose of backing up the official foreign exchange policy would be essential to curtail the power of the 'gnomes'. In the early 'thirties the Exchange Equalisation Account, owing to the inadequacy of its dollar reserves, which were exhausted during the crisis of 1931, was largely at the mercy of speculators. By the late 'thirties, however, it had succeeded in accumulating a sufficiently large reserve to inspire respect in the foreign exchange market. Indeed speculators left sterling alone sometime for months on end owing to the risk of being caught in a bear squeeze.

It is tempting for Central Banks and Governments to intervene mainly for the sake of the satisfaction derived from inflicting losses on speculators. Such punishment of the 'gnomes' does not, however, constitute a deterrent in the long run. Victories over speculators by means of intervention, profitable as they may appear, do not alter the basic causes of the weakness of an exchange. Unless the basic economic situation is improved, speculators will try to attack the currency again and again. Under floating exchanges they would have the maximum of temptation to do so, and in the absence of official intervention they would also have the maximum of opportunity for making a profit. The system of unhindered fluctuations of exchanges is indeed the speculators' paradise.

Intervention can serve the purpose of financial warfare as well as that of international co-operation. Before the war it was mainly used for the purposes of financial warfare, even though in 1936 a Tripartite Agreement was concluded between the United States, Britain and France to limit the scope of such use of their exchange reserves.

In the 'sixties intervention took place to a very large extent in co-operation between the leading countries. Such co-operation became possible because all Governments had the same aim – to maintain existing parities. Statesmen have come to realise that monetary stability, like peace, is indivisible. They had learnt their lesson from the currency chaos that resulted from floating exchanges during the 'thirties. They came to realise that the collapse of the defences of each currency makes the defence of the others more difficult. Hence the desire to co-operate in the defence of any currency which is subject to speculative attack.

Under floating exchanges, on the other hand, there could be little scope for co-operation, because in the majority of instances the interests of Governments would clash. There would be too much temptation to secure advantages at the expense of other countries through a competitive depreciation race. Such advantages as could be secured through deliberate undervaluation would be purely temporary, however, if rival countries also intervened to ensure that their overvalued exchanges should become undervalued. There would be no end to such officially assisted leapfrogging depreciations.

It is true, agreements might conceivably be reached to limit the competitive depreciation races. But any agreed limits to the depreciation race between rival countries would entail disadvantages that differ from the much-denounced disadvantages of fixed parities in degree only. Since it is impossible to calculate equilibrium level, any agreed changes in exchange rates are liable to result in undervaluations and overvaluations. In theory they could be corrected by frequent revisions of the agreed rates. In practice they are more likely to be sought to be corrected – and more than corrected – by a resumption of competitive depreciation. The disadvantages of disequilibrium under floating exchanges which are subject to agreed limitations would not be offset by the advantages that are only enjoyed under stability provided by fixed parities.

The only hope for a resumption of co-ordinated intervention under floating exchanges is that sooner or later Governments would realise the futility of trying to snatch advantages for their country by means of an undervaluation of its currency at the expense of other countries. For one thing, they would discover the elementary arithmetical truth that all currencies cannot be undervalued in terms of all other currencies. They would also discover that such advantages as their country would secure through succeeding for the moment in having an undervalued currency would be purely temporary and that the cost of such temporary gains would prove to be too high. In due course they would realise that unless the depreciation race is made subject to regulations and limitations, it might culminate in a disastrous chaos.

The first step towards a return to common sense would be intervention, not only to check movements that would be disadvantageous to the country directly concerned, but also to check movements that might well force other countries in turn to depreciate their currencies.

Even if the undervaluation of a floating currency is not due to deliberate policy of the authorities concerned but to uncontrolled speculation, unless an effort is made to co-ordinate and moderate exchange movements the Governments would drift into financial warfare. They would realise in due course – as they did in the 'thirties – that they must co-operate. And quite obviously there could be no co-operation without intervention to mitigate exchange movements instead of leaving them at the mercy of unrestrained market influences.

But just as there could be no co-operation without intervention, there could be no intervention without co-operation. It is easy to imagine what would happen if two Governments tried to hold the exchange rate between their countries at two different figures. The 'gnomes' would make many millions by buying that exchange from one Government and selling it to the other. Governments would have to come to terms with each other about the rate at which they would intervene, or they must agree which of them should intervene. The IMF rule under which Governments are not permitted to intervene in each other's currency without permission of the Governments concerned might usefully be applied to intervention under floating exchanges.

An important and highly controversial question is whether intervention should be confined to spot exchanges. Although unlimited support of forward sterling in defence of fixed parities was denounced by Britain's official spokesmen in their evidence before the Radcliffe Committee, it became the official policy between November 1964 and November 1967. It received wholehearted support from a number of economists throughout the 'fifties. They now stand discredited as a result of the failure of the effort to defend sterling by the device of their choice and the high cost of the unsuccessful experiment. Had it not been for the ease with which the credits obtained abroad for the defence of sterling could be supplemented by unlimited support of forward sterling, the Government might have felt impelled to adopt effective measures to balance the economy.

The devaluation of sterling in 1967 inflicted gigantic losses on the Exchange Equalisation Account as a result of its heavy forward sales of dollars. What is more, it is now all but generally realised that the pursuit of the policy had been largely responsible for the creation of a situation in which devaluation had become unavoidable. For the unlimited use of this irresponsible device had enabled the Labour Government to avoid or delay the adoption of unpopular but necessary economic and financial measures in order to strengthen sterling.

One should have thought that after the devaluation of 1967 no expert or pseudo-expert would ever dare to suggest that unlimited intervention in forward exchanges should be resumed under the system of fixed parities. But some of them appear to be toying with the idea of advocating a resumption of unlimited intervention in forward exchanges under floating rates. They do so partly on the ground of their mistaken belief that there would be less speculative pressure under floating exchanges than under fixed parities, because 'exchange rates would be nearer to their trade equilibrium levels'. We tried to show in Chapter 9 that this belief is entirely false.

Before November 1967, over a number of years it was almost impossible to open any journals of learned societies or any bank review without coming across articles arguing the infallibility of the device of defending an exchange by unlimited intervention in the forward exchange market. This belief was held with an incredible degree of cocksureness, mostly by economists who had never been inside a foreign exchange department. Since November 1967 there has not been a single admission by the former crusaders for the unlimited support of forward sterling that they had been mistaken. Hardly any of them even tried to explain away the failure of their favourite device to save the pound. They seem to hope that, if only they kept quiet now, their mistaken advice would fade into oblivion sooner or later, so that they might command sufficient prestige to resume advocating the same device under floating exchanges. Sooner or later politicians might listen once more to their siren songs and allow themselves to be seduced into adopting floating rates, to be applied in conjunction with intervention in forward exchanges. Both devices are calculated to enable irresponsible Governments to avoid facing realities. Between them they would make it possible, for a time, to dispense with the adoption of unpopular measures for the sake of preventing exaggerated depreciations.

No doubt in due course the system of floating exchanges and its advocates would become discredited just as the system of unlimited intervention in forward exchanges and its advocates became discredited after the devaluation of 1967. Possibly some of these advocates may be vaguely aware of the risk they are running, but this does not prevent them from agitating for doing the wrong thing in the wrong way. They agitate for bolstering up the discredited system of the future by combining it with the discredited system of the past.

CHAPTER SIXTEEN

Managed Flexibility

ACCORDING to one of the suggested formulas of flexibility, which does not go as far as the system of floating exchanges, fixed parities should be maintained in theory but should be changed much more frequently in practice. Exchange rates could be adjusted to their ever-changing equilibrium levels whenever disequilibrium causes or threatens to cause major difficulties. Although exchanges would not be allowed to find their own level, they would be adapted in frequent intervals to what the authorities consider – rightly or wrongly – to be their trade equilibrium level.

According to a more extreme formula, the system could be applied empirically; whenever there is buying or selling pressure on the exchange, the authorities would take the line of least resistance and adapt the peg in the direction in which the exchange is pressed, to an extent which they deem sufficient for bringing the pressure to an end. Devaluation and revaluation should be decided as a matter of routine, not on a Cabinet level, not even by the Chancellor of the Exchequer or the Governor of the Bank of England, but by a senior Treasury official on the suggestion of a senior Bank of England official. There would be little difference between such a system and that of floating exchanges with systematic intervention. In the present chapter we are concerned with the less radical formula indicated above. It might mean several changes of parities within a year, though the authorities would still endeavour to keep down the number of changes.

This system could be called the 'adjustable peg', if that term were not already earmarked for the existing Bretton Woods system under which parities can also be adjusted – at any rate in theory – whenever there is fundamental disequilibrium. As it is, we could call it 'managed flexibility'. The difference between the two systems is merely one of degree and emphasis. If the Bretton Woods Agreement were applied in letter and in spirit – at any rate in the spirit in which it was envisaged by Keynes – it could reasonably be named the system of the adjustable peg. But as its critics rightly point out, in practice the peg has not been nearly sufficiently adjustable to deserve that name. Our views about this depend of course on the degree of adjustability we favour.

The system we describe in this chapter would be much less flexible than the system of floating exchanges with official intervention to mitigate fluctuations. Whenever a new parity is fixed, the Government would commit itself to its maintenance, at any rate for the time being, until some change in the situation induces it to fix a new parity. Of course the frequency of changes in the parity would depend on the interpretation of the system by those who would apply it.

Under the system of floating exchanges tempered by intervention, the Government does not commit itself at all to any particular rate, though in practice if a rate is held for some time, it comes to be looked upon as a *de facto* parity. An officially declared policy of maintaining the parity of the moment, as long as this can be done conveniently, might command slightly more confidence, though not much more. But the degree of confidence declines with each change of parity if they follow each other too closely.

Such a system, if it means too frequent changes in parities, would have some of the disadvantages of fixed parities without its compensating advantages. If a peg – whether it is called a parity or not – is maintained for some length of time, prices and wages settle down around it. The authorities are apt to become more and more reluctant to change it the longer it is left unchanged. In due course they might come to feel that they are morally committed to its maintenance even if it necessitates the adoption of some unpleasant measures in its defence. Even so, the possibility of frequent changes of official or unofficial parities would enable them to keep the exchange rates closer to their trade equilibrium level than they are under the present application of the Bretton Woods system.

The trouble is – and we cannot emphasise this sufficiently or repeat it often enough – that there is no means of knowing the whereabouts of the trade equilibrium level, which is always a matter of opinion and a matter of controversy. If even Governments and Central Banks are unable to ascertain the equilibrium level of their exchange in spite of the wealth of factual and statistical information available to them, how could speculators who do not possess such information possibly know when an exchange is at its equilibrium level? All they can do is to take a view about it and act accordingly. Whether that view is right or wrong, it is apt to cause heavy buying or selling pressure if it is held widely.

Admittedly there may be a difference in the degree of distrust by speculators and others in a parity according to whether the authorities had adjusted it recently to what they had rightly or wrongly calculated to be equilibrium level. If a parity was adjusted recently, the market might give it the benefit of the doubt, at any rate for some time, which is more than it is likely to do if an obviously wrong parity were maintained with stubborn determination over a long period.

An essential difference between floating exchanges and frequent changes of parities is that under the latter revaluations are apt to be less frequent than recoveries would be under the floating system. In order to avoid having to devalue too frequently, Governments would be reluctant to revalue unless and until they are quite sure that it would be possible and relatively easy to hold the rate at its revalued level. When buying pressure of their currencies developed, they would be inclined not to allow it to produce its full effect on the exchange rate by revaluing the currency. They would prefer to take advantage of the surplus demand for their currency to accumulate reserves, so as to be in a better position to resist the next spell of selling pressure.

In this respect the position is more or less the same under a system which combines floating rates with intervention. Under both systems it is necessary to maintain a substantial reserve. Under either system, whenever the reserve declines below what is considered to be its safety level and the Government is unwilling to replenish it either by means of a depreciation or by means of borrowing abroad, it has to adopt unpopular monetary, fiscal and economic policy measures to check the pressure on the exchange. It is only under pure floating exchanges with no Government intervention whatsoever that the Government would be able to dispense with reserves or ignore their decline. It would also allow the exchange to appreciate instead of taking advantage of the buying pressure for accumulating a big reserve.

Frequent changes of parities are infinitely preferable to freely floating rates, a system under which adjustment is left at the mercy of unrestrained and largely speculative market influences. In a sense the underlying principle is, however, the same. Under both systems the maintenance of stability is given low priority. Even under managed flexibility the Government would be apt to be reluctant to make sacrifices for the sake of maintaining stability and the reserve would usually be allowed to decline considerably before any decision was made to devalue. It would be allowed to increase considerably before the Government decided to revalue. Possibly conventional monetary policy devices would be used more extensively than under the floating system with official intervention. Changes in exchange rates would be effected more efficiently. The difference bears much similarity to the difference between 'contracting in' and 'contracting out'. Under frequent changes of parities the Government has to take the initiative for changing the peg. Under floating exchanges with intervention the Government has to take the initiative for preventing a change that would occur in the absence of its intervention. Under freely fluctuating exchanges the Government's role is reduced to complete neutrality.

If the peg is maintained over a period during which the

equilibrium level appears to change, speculation is encouraged by expectations of another devaluation. It is discouraged, however, by the uncertainty whether and when that devaluation would take place. Above all, speculators are not in a position to take it for granted – in the way they could under floating exchanges – that by their own action they would necessarily be able to bring about a depreciation. Their power would be greater than it is under the present application of the Bretton Woods system, but it would not be nearly as great as it would be under floating exchanges.

But the system of managed flexibility is in a sense liable to produce an even more one-sided effect than the floating rate. Under the latter, speculators are always able to bring about a recovery. Under the system of adjustable parities they are not necessarily able to bring about a revaluation. It is much easier for a Government to resist buying pressure on its currency than to resist selling pressure, even though the former, too, is apt to become an inconvenient *embarras de richesse*, as is seen from the experience of West Germany during 1968–69. Under flexible parities revaluation is a Government decision, and that decision is always taken with reluctance, because of the ever-present risk that the exchange might once more become vulnerable at its revalued level.

One of the reasons why a system of frequent changes in parities is to be preferred to flexibility under the system of floating exchanges is that it is not nearly as demoralising a form of 'gnomocracy'. But undervalued exchanges would not be adjusted to equilibrium level nearly as freely as they would adjust themselves under floating exchanges. The temptation to acquire power and prosperity through a perennial abnormal export surplus is always difficult to resist. The parity would therefore be much less flexible upwards than downwards.

CHAPTER SEVENTEEN

Broadening the Band

AMONG the variety of projects for floating exchanges, the so-called 'band proposal', under which fixed parities and official limits for permissible exchange movements would continue to exist, but the spread, or band, between support points would be widened, appears to receive the most support in official quarters. Advocates of this system claim that it combines the advantages of both fixed and floating exchanges. It is, however, arguable that in reality it combines to some extent the disadvantages of both.

The idea of broadening the spread between the limits of fluctuations represented by the support points is not new. Among others, Keynes advocated in the inter-war period a deliberate widening of the spread between gold points. During the late 'twenties that spread tended to become narrower, because of the decline in the cost of transport and because speedier air transport reduced the loss of interest on gold in transit. Moreover, as a result of the system of earmarking and releasing gold held on deposit with other Central Banks or with the Bank for International Settlements, there was a possibility that transport costs and loss of interest on gold transfers might disappear altogether. To transfer gold from one account to another without moving it physically costs nothing, so that it became possible for Central Banks, had they wished to do so, to make such transfers whenever the exchanges departed, however fractionally, from their parities.

The reason why Keynes was anxious to reverse the narrowing trend of the spread between gold points was that he was concerned about the situation in which 'every puff of wind' was liable to bring about changes in the monetary reserves, thereby affecting the volume and cost of credit available for industry and commerce. Keynes would have liked to widen the band, and the figure he tentatively suggested shortly before the war was 2 per cent. It is perhaps more than coincidence that, when the statutes of the International Monetary Fund were drafted in 1945 with the active collaboration of Keynes, the limit for spreads between the maximum and minimum support points of exchange rates of member countries in relation to the dollar was fixed at exactly 2 per cent. Actually most members of the International Monetary Fund do not avail themselves to a full extent of their right to allow their exchanges to fluctuate within 1 per cent on either side of their dollar parities. The usual range is about ¾ per cent in either direction, making a total spread of 1½ per cent. For sterling, at its parity of $2.40 after the devaluation of 1967, the spread was between 2.42 and 2.38 instead of the permitted maximum limit of 2.424 to 2.376.

In actual practice the Bank of England usually intervened to support sterling long before it declined to minimum support points, and for a long time the rate of 2.3825 was considered to be its minimum support point. It was not until the summer of 1969 that sterling was allowed to fall slightly below 2.3825.

Since the limit of 2 per cent operates only between the dollar and the currencies of other member countries, this means a permitted maximum limit of 4 per cent between non-dollar currencies – or, on the basis of the *de facto* spread of 1½ per cent, a maximum of 3 per cent. This is because member Governments are under no obligation to intervene to prevent a depreciation of their exchanges in relation to any currency other than the dollar. As a result, when sterling is at its minimum support point in relation to the dollar while the D. mark is at its maximum support point in relation to the dollar, the actual spread for the sterling–D. mark rate is about 3 per cent, while the maximum of spread permitted under the Bretton Woods rules is 4 per cent. This technical point is explained in my *Textbook on Foreign Exchange*.

Support points fixed under the IMF rules and under their application in practice relate to spot rates only. There has never been any attempt to fix a limit for forward rates which, in the absence of intervention, are apt to depreciate or appreciate well beyond support points whenever the maintenance of the parities comes to be doubted. As far as forward rates are concerned, the 'band' has no fixed limits. In actual practice the spread was often 20 per cent and more.

In recent years many suggestions favouring a broadening of the 'band' for spot rates were made from a wide variety of quarters. Opinions to that effect were expressed by authoritative bodies such as the Group of Ten and by the Joint Economic Committee of Congress, and also by prominent individual Central Bankers. Most of them were reluctant to commit themselves as to the extent of the spread, but 4 per cent was the favourite figure. As we shall see later, from the point of view of the case for and against a broadening of the band the difference between broadening it by ½ per cent or by 5 per cent is not a mere matter of degree. Totally different sets of arguments apply for and against the device according to the extent of the proposed broadening.

Many Central Banks are known to be in favour of a moderate widening of the band because it would give them more scope for manœuvring by means of intervention. Another argument in favour of a moderate broadening is that for speculators it would become potentially more profitable to swim against the prevailing speculative tide and more risky to swim with the prevailing speculative tide. As a result, it is argued, the development of two-way speculation might reduce the extent of the one-sided pressure and the extent to which the authorities would have to support their exchange.

This argument is undoubtedly valid if applied to seasonal and other minor movements at a time when parities and support points are trusted. When distrust in the maintenance of parities and support points develops, however, one-sided speculative pressure soon pushes the rates towards their support points, wherever those support points happen to be. If the market is all one-way, and there is a substantial discrepancy between private buying and selling orders, the authorities have to supply the deficiency in order to bridge the gap regardless of the whereabouts of the support points. Mr Roy Bridge, the distinguished head of the foreign exchange department of the Bank of England until 1969, was a case of *nomen est omen*, as his task in life between 1964 and 1967 was to *bridge* the gap between supply and demand in dollars. He had to provide the counterpart, at rates above the minimum support point of $2.78 if possible, or at support point if necessary. It makes no difference whether the minimum support point on the basis of the present parity of $2.40 is at 2.38 or, say, at 2.36. If there is persistent selling pressure, the rate declines to the figure at which the Bank of England is willing to support it or is obliged under IMF rules to support it.

Under the system of broader bands, selling pressure would tend to increase until the rate would actually reach the point at which the authorities resist its further depreciation. Not only those who expect devaluation but many of those who have confidence in the maintenance of existing parities and support points always take a hand for the sake of the small but probable profit that could reasonably be expected in given circumstances even if the rate remains above its lower support point. This means that if the scope of a depreciation within support points increases through a widening of the band, the number of speculators who do not expect a change in the parity, and the extent of their operations, would tend to increase. There would be, for instance, more inducement for speculators to take advantage of anticipated seasonal movements, because profit possibilities on such operations would be increased through a widening of the band. If seasonal and other normal movements tend to become wider, it would be more likely that they might become self-aggravating even if there is initially no acute distrust in parities and support points. A depreciation of sterling by, say, 2 cents might in given circumstances be sufficient to give rise to a wave of pessimism on the assumption that it is the beginning of a major wave of selling pressure.

Admittedly in given situations the possibility of bigger losses on short positions through a recovery of an exchange from a lowered minimum support point to its higher maximum support point is liable to deter speculators from taking the increased risk by acting on their expectation of a fall of the rate to support point. It is liable to induce speculators to act on their expectation of a rise the possible extent of which would be increased by a widening of the gap. But whenever there is a sterling scare, the wideness of the band would fail to produce such an effect, as profit possibilities in case of a change of parities or support points would heavily outweigh fears of limited but calculable losses and hopes of limited but calculable profits with a possibility of much larger profits in case of devaluation.

What advocates of a broader band appear to overlook is that even under the present system of narrow bands profits and losses on speculative operations are not limited by the difference between actual spot rates and support points. Most speculative operations assume the form of forward exchange transactions. And since during periods of one-sided pressure forward rates rise or fall well beyond support points, it is these rates that determine the full extent of the risk for those who swim with the prevailing tide and the full extent of profit possibilities for those who swim against the prevailing tide.

For instance, when spot sterling is right down to its minimum support point, forward sterling may be at a substantial discount of, say, 10 cents for three months, in which case the risk involved in going short in sterling is not determined by its present band of 4 cents but is as much as 14 cents. In theory there is a possibility of a recovery of the spot rate to $2.42, at which rate speculators who had sold forward at $2.28 for three months would have to cover when their forward contracts mature. Those who are optimistic about sterling's prospects and have the courage of their convictions stand a chance of making a much bigger profit than 4 cents even under the existing narrow band if they buy sterling forward at a heavy discount. From this point of view even a substantial broadening of the band would not make such a big difference to speculators and other operators in foreign exchanges as supporters of the band proposals claim it would.

The band proposal has inspired enthusiastic support in many quarters. Professor Halm goes so far in his enthusiasm as to claim that exchange fluctuations within a broadened band would induce 'instant and automatic adjustment in the trade'. We saw earlier that Professor Machlup claims the same result through floating exchanges. This optimism is really amazing. When they talk about *instant* adjustment they overlook the existence of inevitable time-lags between changes in exchange rates and the effects of such changes on imports and exports, and leads and lags on payments for them. Professor Halm disregards rigidities and frictions when he maintains that 'all prices are instantly changed' as a result of exchange movement. His world is not our real world but an ideal world where prices, imports and exports behave in accordance with rules laid down by textbooks on economics written before the existence and influence of elasticities and rigidities came to be realised.

Professor Halm admits that he regards the band proposal as the first step towards freely floating exchanges. Once the band system has operated successfully for some time, it might be possible, according to him, to drop both limits and managements within limits – and live happily ever after. His candid admission has confirmed my suspicion that the band proposal is really meant to be the thin end of the wedge. Those who advocate it want to lure the unwary towards the system of floating rates by first putting forward a much less radical proposal. Many of those who would not think of endorsing the proposal for floating exchanges might not resist the band proposal which appears to maintain the principle of fixed parities. The wider the band, the nearer is the system to that of floating exchanges. Hence the importance of the difference between a proposal to widen the band to 4 per cent and a proposal to widen it to 10 per cent or to 20 per cent.

Supporters of the band proposal, like those of freely floating exchanges, contend that under their system exchange fluctuations would obviate the necessity for monetary policy measures affecting the domestic economy. According to them, exchange movements would automatically produce all the effect that is produced today by domestic monetary policy devices. Even if we accepted that claim it would have to be regarded as an argument against the system and not one for it. Exaggerated trends in the domestic economy have to be regulated by monetary policy measures if we want to avoid runaway booms and disastrous slumps. If the band proposal were to be adopted for the sake of avoiding measures that would keep booms under control and prevent them from developing into self-aggravating inflationary booms, so much the worse for the band proposal. It is clearly absurd to recommend that device as a substitute for conventional monetary policy devices of the kind that have safeguarded the world against runaway booms for a quarter of a century, even if they were unable to safeguard us against creeping inflation.

Exchange fluctuations within a broad band that would take the place of monetary, economic and fiscal counter-cyclical measures would aggravate the prevailing exaggerated trend. A depreciation of the exchange of a country which is in difficulties owing to domestic inflation would not solve its problem – it would amount to pouring oil on the fire of inflation.

If the extent to which the band is broadened is very moderate, it is a technical device which may have its points. It would facilitate effective intervention to some slight extent as it would provide more opportunities for the authorities to penalise speculators, especially those who buy spot exchanges and intend to cover before delivery is due in two days. But it would be a mistake to attach too much importance to this argument. Anyhow, victories over speculators are no substitute for the pursuit of sound policies aimed at reducing their power for evil by achieving and maintaining a sound economy and a strong currency.

If the extent of broadening the band is substantial – if, for instance, it is of the order of 10 per cent on each side of the parities – then in practice the system thus created would amount to floating exchanges with limits. Even these limits could not be depended upon. Once the broadening exceeds the modest limits of a technical adjustment for tactical purposes and, through its large extent, comes to serve requirements of broad strategy, the possibility of repeating the exercise could not be ruled out. If it should be decided that selling pressure on sterling should be met by lowering its minimum support point to, say, $2.20, it would become necessary to envisage the possibility of its further lowering to $2.00 or even below, in face of continued pressure. All arguments against floating exchanges would apply to the proposal for such a considerable broadening of the band.

It has been suggested that the International Monetary Fund's member Governments, in return for the permission to broaden the band, should give a solemn undertaking that in no circumstances would they allow the exchanges to go beyond the broader limits to be authorised by the IMF. There is no reason to believe, however, that in case of persistent pressures member Governments would necessarily abstain from changing their parities or broadening the band even further, with or without the consent of the IMF. In circumstances in which they are now prepared to dishonour their pledge – as France did in 1969 – not to lower their parities without approval by the IMF, there is no reason whatsoever to suppose that they would consider their new pledge sacrosanct merely because the figures of the support points have been changed.

Anyhow, the chances are that we shall soon witness a moderate broadening of the band. Whether it will be followed in due course by a more substantial broadening remains to be seen. What is essential is to realise that a success of the minor adjustment would not prove the case in favour of a major adjustment.

CHAPTER EIGHTEEN

The Undynamic Crawling Peg

IF a working party of top-ranking economists were to set out to elaborate a system which would get the worst of every possible world by combining all the disadvantages of the rigid system with those of the flexible system without any of their redeeming features, they could do no better than recommend the 'crawling peg' scheme. Very appropriately, a horrid system has been given a horrid name. Recently efforts were made to rename it the 'dynamic peg' – presumably because of its essentially undynamic character.

The basic idea of that system is that parities should not be changed suddenly but very gradually. Instead of devaluing or revaluing to the extent of 10 per cent or 20 per cent with one swift stroke, advocates of this system suggest that changes in parities should be carried out at a rate of, say, 2 per cent p.a., in monthly or preferably weekly instalments of minute fractions of 1 per cent. It is a kind of economic homeopathy aiming at curing an acute and dangerous disease, calling for drastic and urgent remedies, by a very gradual administration of diminutive doses of medicine over a very long period.

It would be difficult to imagine any process less dynamic than the slow-motion picture of an exchange parity crawling downwards or upwards at the rate of, say, $0.0001 per week. Of course it is quite understandable if the authors and supporters of the scheme have come to realise, somewhat belatedly, that the unfortunate choice of its name is liable to kill the scheme with ridicule. What is less easy to understand is that the result of their second choice should be such an absurd misnomer which, in a different way, is fully as comic as the name it is meant to erase from our memory.

The authors of the scheme aim at relaxing the rigidity of our system, and at mitigating the shocks of major devaluations or revaluations, by providing for very gradual crawling devaluations and revaluations. It is somewhat puzzling how any one can possibly work up any enthusiasm for a system under which, during the first twelve months after an urgently needed change was decided upon, the extent of imbalance which it is intended to correct would be only slightly more moderate than it was before the series of adjustments of the exchange rate. Movements under crawling parities would be hardly wider than ordinary exchange movements that take place within existing fixed support points.

The question is, do advocates of the device intend it for correcting a major disequilibrium or merely for correcting a very moderate disequilibrium? If they want to correct major overvaluations or undervaluations, the crawl would have to proceed over a number of years and the remedy would be completely ineffective, at any rate during the first few years. It would only stand a chance of becoming effective towards the end of the long-drawn out 'crawl'. As for the use of the device for the correction of some minor disequilibrium, it is hardly worth while to unsettle existing parities for the sake of eliminating small discrepancies the existence of which is in any case bound to be largely a matter of opinion.

For the equilibrium level of an exchange rate cannot be reckoned in terms of 1 per cent or 2 per cent. Such a minor disequilibrium could not possibly be ascertained, and it is always a matter of opinion whether it exists at all. As pointed out earlier, the calculations of the equilibrium level of exchanges is very far from being an exact science. There is apt to be a margin of error of the order of 5 per cent or even of 10 per cent in either direction. In itself the fact that an exchange is persistently weak does not necessarily mean that it is overvalued. Its weaknesses may be caused by a variety of influences entirely or largely independent of any discrepancy between the exchange rate and its trade equilibrium level.

Even a perennial import surplus or a perennial export

surplus does not necessarily indicate the existence of disequilibrium. It may be caused by a wide variety of influences unrelated to the purchasing-power parities of the exchange concerned. An adverse balance or a favourable balance has to persist over a fairly long period before its existence could be accepted as indicating the possibility of an undervaluation of the exchange. Nor is a persistent buying pressure or selling pressure on a currency acceptable as a conclusive evidence of undervaluation, as it may be caused by capital movements, or by a wide variety of causes unrelated to an undervaluation of the exchange that is under pressure.

There is bound to be a time-lag between the development of a disequilibrium and the realisation of its existence with a sufficient degree of certainty to justify drastic corrective action in the form of a change in the parity. The crawling peg system proposes to prolong that inevitable time-lag deliberately through the slow pace with which corrective action is taken. The equilibrium level is liable to change very considerably and at times very suddenly during the years while the 'crawl' is in progress. In the course of twelve months the overvaluation or undervaluation of a currency is liable to change by anything up to 5 per cent or more. For instance, within a few weeks in May–June 1968 the French franc changed to that extent. A formerly overvalued currency might become undervalued in a very short time, or vice versa.

If an attempt is made to correct an assumed disequilibrium by moving the peg gradually to the extent of, say, 4 per cent in two years, during the course of those two years the equilibrium level of that currency is liable to change upwards or downwards by a great deal more than 4 per cent. After the adjustment the disequilibrium might well be found to be just as wide as it was before the adjustment. It might be twice as wide. Or there might develop a disequilibrium in the opposite sense.

Under the proposed system it would take five years or more to correct a disequilibrium of 10 per cent, a degree of disequilibrium that is liable to be encountered even in the absence of any abnormal developments. During the greater part of the period of the 'crawl' all or most disadvantages of a disequilibrium arising from rigid exchanges would continue to operate to the detriment of the economy of the country concerned, albeit to a slowly diminishing extent.

Assuming an initial overvaluation of an exchange by, say, 10 per cent, and assuming for the sake of argument that during the process of the crawl at the rate of 2 per cent p.a. the relative price level of the two countries would remain unchanged, it would take fully five years for the balance to be restored. But the second assumption is not realistic, since the depreciation of the exchange, and the knowledge that its depreciation was intended to continue, would stimulate the rise of the domestic price level in the country with an overvalued currency. The downward crawl of the exchange value of that currency will itself change the ratio between the price levels of the countries concerned.

If in 1970 the domestic price level in the country concerned is 100, while that of the other country is 90, as a result of the downward crawl of the exchange at the rate of 2 per cent p.a. the domestic price level of the first country will have risen to well over 100 – perhaps to 103 or 104 – by 1975, so that the discrepancy between the price levels will have risen from 10 to 13 or 14. The depreciation of the currency by 10 per cent would reduce the disequilibrium from 10 to 3 or 4, but would not eliminate it altogether. Meanwhile throughout the five years while the disequilibrium is slowly reduced, the adverse trade balance due to the overvaluation of the currency would continue on a diminishing scale. Only towards the end of the period would the process result in an appreciable increase of exports and an appreciable decline of imports. Meanwhile interest rates would have to be kept abnormally high to defend the overvalued currency. The adverse balance might even become accentuated by the anticipation of a further rise in prices, especially in those of imported goods.

The length of the periods of adjustment envisaged by the advocates of the crawling peg would mean that long before the disequilibrium is eliminated the reserves would become exhausted or at any rate reduced below danger level, and external indebtedness would have to be increased. To mitigate such adverse changes, the Government would have to resort to defensive measures similar to those applied under the system of fixed parities. Indeed from this point of view the difference between a rigid system and the system of the crawling peg is at best one of degree. But should the psychological effects of the crawling peg prove to be as unfavourable as it seems reasonable to expect them to be, the defence of the gradually lowered parities would necessitate even larger reserves or foreign credits, even tougher conventional monetary, economic and fiscal devices, and even more stringent exchange restrictions than the defence of fixed parities.

There is no reason whatsoever to imagine for a moment that, once the system of the crawling peg is adopted, speculators and others concerned with foreign exchanges would hold their hands until the balance of payments deficit is supposed to become removed eventually. If speculators expect, rightly or wrongly, to make a profit of, say, between 15 and 25 per cent by going short in a devaluation-prone currency, a reduction of their profit prospect by a fraction of 1 per cent every week or every month is not likely to induce them to abstain from their speculative operations. Indeed, the fact that the Government deemed it necessary to set the crawling process in motion would be generally interpreted as an official confirmation of the existence of a disequilibrium and an announcement of the Government's intention to correct it by a reduction in the value of the exchange concerned.

Nor is there any reason to suppose that the parity would be trusted after the weekly and monthly adjustments by fractions of 1 per cent, or even after the completion of, say, 2 per cent of the projected adjustment of 10 per cent. When Germany revalued the D. mark in 1961 by as much as 5 per cent, it only stimulated expectations of a further upward adjustment. The same thing happened in the opposite sense after the devaluation of sterling in 1967 and of the franc in 1969. An inadequate degree of devaluation or revaluation – or even a devaluation or revaluation that is not obviously adequate – defeat is its immediate object because it weakens confidence in the Government's determination to defend its parity, while it falls short of bringing about a sufficient material or psychological improvement to correct the imbalance. And under the crawling peg the extent of the revaluation or devaluation is intended to be kept deliberately and obviously inadequate for a number of years. After the adjustments of the parities of sterling, the franc and the D. mark the Governments concerned made some effort to obviate the need for further adjustments. Under the crawling peg it would be the Government's declared intention to make further adjustments.

For some inscrutable reason, advocates of the crawling peg postulate that a moderate adjustment of the peg to the extent of a bare fraction of the disequilibrium would inspire confidence in the adjusted peg. Yet there is no reason whatsoever to assume that anyone except advocates of the crawling peg would trust the new parities. For one thing, the demoralising effect of any form of increased flexibility would make it more difficult to make a firm stand at any parity. Many holders of balances in currencies condemned to gradual depreciation would withdraw their balances. The extent of the crawling depreciation of the exchanges would be regarded as a negative interest rate.

Advocates of the plan suggest that foreign holders of balances should be compensated for their capital losses resulting from the gradual depreciation of their holdings through being allowed higher interest rates. This might satisfy holders who have no intention of covering the exchange risk, but the majority of holders would want to cover. That being so, their decision whether to retain the balances would depend as much on forward rates as on interest rates. Higher interest rates for the sake of retaining uncovered balances, coupled with anticipation of a depreciation of the currency would make for a widening of the forward discount. This would increase the cost of covering the exchange risk.

Holders and also speculators would discount future adjustments months ahead. In any case the adoption of such a puerile system would inspire a wave of distrust, and devaluation on a larger scale would be widely anticipated. If sterling is distrusted at $2.38, is there any reason to suppose that it would command confidence at $2.3799, or at $2.3798, or at $2.3797, etc.? Would a pledge that its depreciation would never become accelerated inspire confidence? Even the most solemn undertaking that a parity would be defended 'with the last drop of our blood' (to quote Mussolini's famous promise) commands very little respect in our cynical age. The moment the policy of determined resistance to pressure on currency is abandoned, the possibility of further retreat would come to be regarded not as a mere possibility but as a probability, in given circumstances.

It may well be asked whether it would be worth while to interefere with fixed parities for the sake of making the fractional changes proposed by the advocates of the crawling peg. The chances are that, under increased speculative pressure and owing to prolonged delay in the adjustment of an openly acknowledged disequilibrium, the crawl might have to be accelerated into a walk at slow pace and later into a walk at a more rapid pace and eventually into a run. Or it might have to be followed by a jump in the form of devaluation or revaluation. Anyhow many people would suspect it to be the thin edge of the wedge, in the same way as they would suspect a broadening of the band.

The crawling peg proposal bears some similarity to the monetary reform that was actually put into operation during the inter-war depression in the small Austrian town of Wörgl. Under the system advocated by Silvio Gesell – quoted at length by Keynes in his *General Theory of Employment, Interest and Money* – the notes issued by the municipal authorities of that town were depreciated to the extent of a small percentage every week by making it compulsory for holders to affix a weekly stamp on them. For this reason, instead of hoarding the notes, the recipients hastened to spend them as soon as possible by putting their purchases forward. The result was increased demand leading to increased production, for the benefit of the entire community.

This experiment was justified amidst the prevailing deflationary depression, when the root of the trouble was inadequate demand and underconsumption. But today countries the exchanges of which tend to depreciate owing to an import surplus caused by creeping inflation suffer from overconsumption and not from underconsumption. It is surely absurd to expect that a further stimulus given to overconsumption by a gradual depreciation of the currency would correct the disequilibrium. On the contrary it stands to reason that the disequilibrium would tend to become accentuated, because the anticipation of its further depreciation would stimulate consumer demand. Advocates of the crawling peg are like incompetent doctors who prescribe for patients with a high blood-pressure a treatment that is effective against low blood-pressure. Men have been certified insane for less than that.

It may be argued that, since prices are rising in any case, the accentuation of their increase as a result of a slow deliberate depreciation of the exchange would be a mere matter of degree. But it would make quite a difference if the domestic purchasing power of a currency, instead of depreciating by, say, 5 per cent p.a., would come to be depreciating at 7 per cent p.a. And, while its present depreciation takes place in spite of the official policy aiming at preventing it, the additional depreciation would form part of an openly declared official policy. For this reason alone its adverse effect on consumer demand, and therefore on exports and imports, would be more pronounced than that of the prevailing unintended rise in prices which the Government is unable to prevent.

If a strong currency, instead of being revalued, is gradually raised in value through the application of the crawling peg system in an upward direction, holders of such a currency would be reluctant to part with it, owing to the prospects of its appreciation. This means that the operation of the system would tend to restrict consumer spending so that the disequilibrium of the undervalued currency in relation to other currencies would become wider. This would mean even larger export surpluses at the expense of countries with overvalued currencies, in spite of microscopic reductions in the extent to which their currencies are overvalued. 'Whosoever hath, to him shall be given, but whosoever hath not, from him shall be taken away even that he hath' should be the motto of 'crawlers' when advocating their favourite device as a substitute for straight revaluation of undervalued currencies.

Apart altogether from any other considerations the adoption of such a silly system is bound to inspire distrust in the competence of the Government that adopts it and therefore in its ability to carry out its ill-conceived policy successfully. On balance, it may be found that adoption of the crawling peg system, so far from reducing the likelihood of drastic changes of parities, tends to increase it. Indeed it is even conceivable that adoption of the crawling peg would increase the overvaluation or undervaluation of currencies to a higher degree than the rate at which exchange rates are permitted to crawl towards their equilibrium level. And speculative pressure would tend to increase rather than decline.

In most of the above criticisms of the crawling peg I merely stated the obvious. Nevertheless it is possible that the IMF will give the absurd scheme its blessing by authorising member-Governments to apply it within the limits of 10 per cent on either side of their original parities – possibly on either side of their new authorised parities. Such a decision would go a long way towards discrediting the IMF even more than its attitude towards buying South African gold has already discredited it. The obvious partiality with which it twisted its rules concerning its obligation to buy gold has undermined its moral authority. It could ill afford a further loss of prestige through a display of sheer incompetence in endorsing a system so obviously idiotic as the crawling peg.

CHAPTER NINETEEN

Improving the Existing System

ADMITTEDLY it is easy to find fault with the reform proposals made by others. It would be incomparably more difficult to make a counter-proposal suggesting a bold, imaginative and original reform that would be economically satisfactory, politically acceptable and technically feasible. It is not the object of this book to try to perform that task. But there *is* an alternative to their plans which is worth considering, even though it is neither original nor ingenious – the Bretton Woods system should be maintained but its interpretation and application should be improved. There must be a great deal of re-thinking on those lines.

One of the main improvements would be to apply it in the same spirit in which it had been conceived. The authors of the plan envisaged it as a system which would possess a moderate degree of flexibility. Keynes was criticised during the controversy over Bretton Woods – I must confess to have been one of the critics – for lending his authority to a scheme which, it was contended, would amount virtually to a return to a new form of the gold standard. His main argument in answer to his critics was that under the Bretton Woods system the countries adopting it would be entitled to devalue up to 10 per cent without having to ask anyone's permission, and that permission for larger changes of parities would be given in case of fundamental disequilibrium. He and other authors of the scheme had taken it for granted that the Governments of the countries associated with the International Monetary Fund would make full use of the escape clauses that had been inserted in order to mitigate the rigidity of fixed parities.

In practice, as we saw earlier, the Governments of most

leading countries showed themselves extremely reluctant to avail themselves of their right to devalue or revalue. The fact that there were relatively few devaluations between 1946 and 1969 was due, not to the unwillingness of the IMF to authorise them, but to the unwillingness of member Governments to ask for authorisation to devalue to an extent in excess of the permitted limit, and even to devalue to an extent that would require no authorisation.

Possibly the explanation of this reluctance to devalue during the early years of the operation of the scheme was that there was a world-wide scarcity of goods. There was a sellers' market in the late 'forties and even countries with an overvalued currency found it easy to export. Most Governments preferred, therefore, to have an overvalued exchange rather than an undervalued exchange that would encourage exports and would discourage imports, resulting in 'unrequited exports' – a new term coined in a new situation in which most countries aimed at avoiding an aggravation of their shortages of goods through exporting in excess of their imports.

Another reason why overvalued exchanges were preferred to undervalued exchanges was that the former meant favourable terms of trade. Countries with overvalued currencies obtained more imports in exchange for the same amount of exports. Although by the end of the 'forties, or at any rate by the early 'fifties, after the end of the war in Korea, wartime scarcities and scarcities created by reconstruction of war damage were more or less made good, the spirit of reluctance to devalue that prevailed during the immediate post-war years continued to prevail. Prevention of devaluation became a matter of prestige. Most Governments of the leading industrial countries – once they succeeded in overcoming their post-war difficulties that had repeatedly forced some of them to devalue very much against their wishes – came to be determined to resist pressure to devalue.

There was even stronger reluctance by Governments to revalue undervalued exchanges. They had the right to revalue, but very seldom exercised it. The Bretton Woods system meant in practice an even higher degree of rigidity against revaluations than against devaluation.

The maintenance of the existing IMF parities is looked upon as a supreme duty, just as the maintenance of gold parities had been looked upon under the gold standard. In a sense this is as it should be. Had Governments given way to adverse pressure too easily, the system of relative monetary stability established by the Bretton Woods Agreement would have ended long before now. It is of course an extremely difficult task to steer halfway between the Scylla of undue rigidity and the Charybdis of undue flexibility. From the point of view of maintaining the Bretton Woods system, it is equally important to avoid getting into a mentality that changes of parities don't matter, and to avoid getting into a mentality that such changes must be prevented at all costs regardless of the extent of any prevailing fundamental disequilibrium.

In accordance with the Bretton Woods spirit, efforts ought to be made in the first instance to restore equilibrium not by adjustments of the parities but by hard and honest efforts to reduce or keep down prices and domestic demand in deficit countries. Surplus countries too are expected to contribute their share towards restoring equilibrium by pursuing a policy of expansion that would correct the balance of payments. Should surplus countries not be prepared to inflate in order to mitigate the overvaluation of their currencies, member countries of the IMF could be authorised by the IMF to make more use of the 'scarce currency clause' contained in the Bretton Woods Agreement and embodied in the IMF rules. Under that clause the IMF could and should declare the currency of the offending surplus country scarce and members would be authorised to discriminate against that country. But the definition of circumstances in which this could be done was interpreted so strictly that there was no opportunity during nearly a quarter of a century while the IMF was in existence to apply it in a single instance. Yet the dollar was definitely scarce most of the time during the first ten years after the establishment of the IMF, and the D. mark was definitely scarce most of the time since the late 'fifties. But technically the extent and circumstances of their scarcity did not correspond to the letter of the relevant rule.

Had the definition of scarce currencies been less narrow, in these instances the deficit countries would have been at liberty to apply discriminatory trade and exchange control measures against the surplus countries. The mere possibility of such measures might have made their actual application unnecessary, because surplus countries, rather than expose themselves to discriminatory restrictions, would probably have made a greater effort to restore equilibrium with the aid of domestic monetary policy measures, by encouraging imports and discouraging exports to a sufficient extent, or by revaluing their currencies.

In the form in which it was adopted and interpreted, the scarce currency clause proved to be quite worthless. In substance it merely means that countries which have absolutely no supplies in the scarce currency concerned and are absolutely unable to secure any supplies of such currency might conceivably be permitted to take steps that would enable them not to spend their non-existent currencies on the goods of the country the currency of which is declared scarce. In the course of one of my controversies over this point, in the pages of *The Banker* in 1946, I said that this rule read like *Alice in Wonderland*. For there was even a possibility of situations in which a deficit country would remain technically under obligation to continue to spend the surplus country's currency without limitation, although it possessed none and was unable to obtain any.

In the meantime the significance of a scarce currency clause, even if it were effective in theory and if it were strictly enforced in practice, has become reduced by the development of international co-operation between monetary authorities and by the revival of international lending and borrowing on an unprecedented scale. Owing to the ease with which deficit countries can obtain assistance from the IMF or from foreign Central Banks, or can borrow in the Euro-currency market and in the Euro-bond market, the likelihood of real scarcity developing in hard currencies has become greatly reduced. The re-cycling of unwanted 'hot money' by surplus countries and the adoption of Special Drawing Rights and other devices of co-operation between Central Banks – directly or through the intermediary of the IMF and the BIS – aims at removing the development of scarce currency situations in a sense envisaged by the authors of the Bretton Woods plan.

As a result of the overdose of international co-operation experienced in recent years, deficit countries are in a position to continue to inflate, leaving it to surplus countries to re-lend their surpluses on their balances of payments. Another objection to excessive financial assistance to deficit countries is that the expansion of international resources steps up the pace of world inflation. There is much to be said against placing the task of readjusting disequilibrium entirely or even overwhelmingly on the surplus countries' shoulders, making it their duty to reduce their surpluses or to re-lend them to the deficit countries. The behaviour of deficit countries in 1968–69 in trying to induce Germany to revalue the D. mark was like a demand by sick people that a healthy person should take their medicine.

When a disequilibrium is too marked, situations are liable to arise in which changes of parities become an infinitely smaller evil than the degree of deflation or inflation required in order to avoid this. But it has become a habit to regard parities which were maintained over a period of years as sacrosanct. A middle course between that attitude and the irresponsible mentality by which parities could and should be cheerfully changed as a matter of course each time there is pressure on the exchange is yet to be found. Fortunately a devaluation is still widely regarded as an admission of defeat. But it is an admission which ought to be made more readily when the defeat becomes obviously inevitable. Deficit countries should then face reality.

It is unfortunate that considerations of political popularity and prestige are often regarded as more important than vital interests that are apt to be jeopardised by prolonged resistance to inevitable devaluation or revaluations. To improve on the operation of the Bretton Woods system it would be necessary to break down that attitude and strike a balance between excessive rigidity and undue elasticity. But if it is right to regard devaluation as a defeat which must be avoided if possible, it is equally right to regard revaluation as a victory of which surplus countries should feel proud as a great achievement instead of avoiding it at all costs.

The ideal way in which both undue rigidity and undue elasticity could be mitigated would be by arranging from time to time an agreed reconsideration of parities and their realignment, if necessary, under the auspices of the IMF. Most Governments would be then not nearly as reluctant to adjust their parities if a number of other Governments acted likewise at the same time, for they would not be exposed to anything like the same extent of criticism as in the case of an isolated adjustment of their parities.

The practical difficulty about this solution is that, in order to agree on the terms of realignments, the Governments would have to engage in lengthy and difficult negotiations. Information would be bound to leak out, and long before the Governments are ready to sign there would be sweeping waves of speculation anticipating the impending changes of parities. The way to avoid this would be to rush through the negotiations in the course of a long weekend which could be prolonged by a day or two of 'bank holiday', during which the foreign exchange markets and Stock Exchanges remained closed.

Of course it is inconceivable that all Governments, or even the most important Governments, would come to terms about changes of parities in a matter of days. Any attempt to achieve agreed realignment might degenerate into interminable haggling in which political considerations would play a more important part than economic and financial considerations. And the chances are that the result would be a compromise determined usually according to the number of trumps each Government holds rather than by the vital requirements of equilibrium. The Governments that would hold most of the trumps would have their way, while Governments in weaker bargaining positions would have to make the best of a bad bargain.

A practicable solution – which would of course be far from being an ideal solution – would be that after the closing of Friday's foreign exchange markets the Government of one of the major countries should simply inform the other Governments about its unilateral decision to devalue its exchange to such-and-such an extent. Other Governments would then have to adapt their parities willy-nilly to the change before the markets reopen on the following Monday.

Amidst conditions prevailing during the 'sixties and which are likely to continue during the 'seventies, an all-round increase in the price of gold would have had to accompany a realignment of parities. Since the United States persists in keeping down the official price of gold at $35 an ounce, other Governments continue to be reluctant to devalue. But if the dollar should be devalued simultaneously with a realignment, they would all feel that they would be in good company.

It is outside the scope of this book to examine the formidable list of arguments for and against an increase in the official American price of gold. For our present purposes it is sufficient to point out that a reasonably substantial increase in the American price would be certain to be followed by an all-round devaluation of the leading currencies. The extent of these devaluations would not be uniform, and this would result in a drastic realignment. It would be politically easier for, say, France to devalue the franc by, say, 55 per cent if at the same time the dollar were cut by 50 per cent than to devalue the franc by another 5 per cent in the absence of any devaluation of the dollar.

One of the arguments in favour of raising the American price of gold is that it would result in a much more natural increase in international liquidity than through the creation of Special Drawing Rights or through the implementation of any of the ingenious proposals put forward to create liquid reserves. Apart from writing up the book-keeping value of the gold reserves, their amount would increase considerably as a result of the stimulus given to gold mining, and even more through a large-scale de-hoarding of gold. This happened during the early 'thirties when the devaluation of the dollar and the depreciation of sterling induced hoarders in India and other countries to take their profits. It was happening during the late 'sixties in respect of silver as a result of the rise in its price. If silver were still a monetary matal, this de-hoarding would have increased international liquidity.

One of the main arguments against raising the price of gold is that the allocation of the additional liquid resources would be far from equitable or convenient. Holders of small gold reserves would get little, even though they need the additional resources much more than the more fortunate countries which are in possession of large reserves. But if the operation is accompanied by a realignment of parities, it might provide an opportunity for a gradual redistribution of the monetary gold stock and of other international reserves. This argument would only be valid, however, if the countries with small reserves which devalue to a higher degree would not rely excessively on the resulting undervaluation of their currencies to solve their balance of payments problem. As the example of two British devaluations since the end of the Second World War and of the French devaluation of 1969 seem to indicate, devaluation does not in itself solve everything. Countries which devalued must work not less hard but harder, and they must practise not less self-restraint but more self-restraint. This is how Britain derived benefit from the depreciation of sterling in 1931.

Those who complain about the inadequacy of international liquid reserves seem to have overlooked the painfully obvious fact that world prices have been rising ever since the Second World War. Judging by that fact, it seems that liquid resources have been more than adequate. They have been sufficient to finance an increasing volume of international trade at increasingly high prices. The development and expansion of the Euro-currency markets has added tens of billions of dollars to the volume of international liquid resources.

Admittedly these additional resources make it much easier to speculate in devaluation-prone or revaluation-prone currencies, so that they constitute a potential cause of instability which has increased reserve requirements for emergencies. But the development of the Euro-bond market has gone a long way towards mitigating this disadvantage by contributing towards a consolidation of liquid Euro-currency liabilities. Both markets have immense possibilities. They have both contributed, however, towards increasing the volume of international financial liabilities, and they have therefore increased the need for international reserves in emergencies, while increasing liquid resources for normal requirements. Their expansion has further increased the potential instability.

The adoption of the proposal providing for Special Drawing Rights by the IMF is widely regarded as an important step in the desired direction. There is room, however, for two opinions on this subject. As a result of these large additions to the volume of international credits, the credit structure will become even less stable than it was before the adoption of Special Drawing Rights. The system would not stand the test of a major crisis. It would be an infinitely preferable way of increasing international liquidity to raise the American price of gold, because as a result of such an operation the foundations of the international credit structure would be strengthened through an increase in the amount of gold reserves.

It would be idle to expect the adoption of floating exchanges to contribute towards a solution of the problem of international liquidity. Indeed most of its advocates regard it as an alternative to an increase in the volume of liquid reserves. While a satisfactory realignment of parities would go a long way towards solving the problem of liquidity by reducing the need for large liquid reserves for the defence of overvalued currencies, floating exchanges would produce exactly the opposite effect. We saw in Chapter 13 that the distrust generated by wild fluctuations of exchange rates would greatly increase the volume of requirements for forward exchange facilities at the same time as reducing the volume of forward exchange facilities available. This would mean that a high proportion of foreign trade which is covered against exchange risk by forward exchange transactions would have to be covered by spot transactions. The resulting increase in foreign currency requirements would itself entail higher requirements of liquid international reserves, even if the monetary authorities abstained from intervening in order to offset speculative pressure. If floating exchanges should be officially supported – as they were in the 'thirties – this would necessitate larger reserves than under fixed parities. In Britain the Exchange Equalisation Account deemed it necessary to accumulate a very large reserve before the war. From this point of view the adoption of floating exchanges would be apt to create a new problem instead of solving the existing one.

We have already pointed out that a dollar devaluation would provide an opportunity for a realistic realignment of parities. Above all, the operation would greatly strengthen the financial power of the United States. As a result of ill-advised policies leading to a considerable reduction of the American gold reserve and to a considerable increase to the external short-term liabilities, the financial power of the United States declined considerably in the 'sixties. This caused grave concern in the free world. It was a great mistake on the part of the American authorities to allow their reserve position to weaken to such an extent simply because they were not prepared either to adopt adequate measures to check the process of deterioration or to carry out the necessary degree of devaluation. As a result of this financial weakening of the country on the strength of which the defence of the free world largely depends, the position of the free world has become much more precarious. This aspect of the subject is even more important than international financial stability or economic growth.

Earlier we repeatedly pointed out another disadvantage of the Bretton Woods system in the way it has been operating, especially during the 'sixties. It has given rise to an overdose of international financial co-operation. This may sound paradoxical. Surely everybody wants to see closer co-operation across the frontiers, and the stability of exchanges since the war has contributed considerably towards the encouraging of such co-operation. Unfortunately there is another side to the picture. In some countries at any rate the ease with which a bad Government is now able to obtain external assistance has bred an irresponsible spirit. The willingness of monetary authorities and private holders of dollars to finance the trade deficit of the United States and the unwarranted extent of American investment abroad has been largely responsible for the reluctance of the American authorities to take the necessary measures to stop the decline of their international financial strength.

A new vocabulary has been invented. In our days if a bad debtor is unable to pay and is unwilling to make an effort to recover its ability to pay so that its creditors have to grant it a willy-nilly moratorium, this is called 're-phasing'. If that selfsame bad debtor is authorised by its creditor to help itself to more loans, this is called 're-cycling'. Special Drawing Rights which are given away, and for the redemption of which no Government is responsible are called 'paper gold'.

The Bretton Woods system, or indeed any conceivable international monetary system, could not be made to work satisfactorily unless this phoney vocabulary is abandoned and the attitude it indicates is changed. It is not the formula that matters but the spirit in which the formula is applied. The process of demoralisation, which is most strikingly evident in Britain but exists in many other countries to some degree, has to be halted and reversed before the world can hope to achieve prosperity combined with stability.

Since ours is not an ideal world, it would be idle to try and find an ideal solution. The solution which would give the world at any rate a chance to straighten out its international monetary problems would be a substantial general alignment of parities on the basis of an increase in the American price of gold. It would not be a once-for-all solution. But, like the dollar devaluation of 1934, it would enable the free world to have some decades of breathing space, with a comparative safety from relapsing into currency chaos. In our imperfect world we could hardly expect more than that.

The adoption of floating exchanges would aggravate the problem of liquidity instead of relieving it because it would inspire distrust in each currency in turn. In due course the dollar would follow sterling in floating downwards. It is true, the D. mark might be floating upwards in spite of its revaluation in 1969. But sooner or later its uncontrolled self-aggravating appreciation would become exaggerated and a stage would be reached at which it would become considered overvalued and therefore vulnerable.

On the other hand, in due course the dollar, and even sterling, might become obviously undervalued and would therefore come to inspire confidence, at any rate in the short run. This would mean that Central Banks and other holders of foreign currency reserves, in order to safeguard their interests, would have to switch their reserves from one currency to another. They would have to engage in shifting of official 'hot money' and in speculation on a gigantic scale to replace their holdings of currencies which have become overvalued by currencies which have become undervalued. Such operations would have to be made at frequent intervals, owing to the wide fluctuations of floating exchange rates and to the ever-changing nature and extent of their disequilibrium.

Exchange guarantees, on the lines of those granted in 1968 by Britain to Sterling Area Governments and Central Banks holding sterling reserves, would be no solution. They would have to be granted on a gigantic scale. The temptation to repudiate such pledges in the way the gold clause was repudiated by the United States after the suspension of the gold standard in 1933 would be very strong if the exchange rates should float strongly against the guarantor.

The logical outcome of the adoption of the floating system would be the disappearance of the gold exchange standard, as most monetary authorities, and also private holders of foreign currencies, would prefer in times of crises to hold gold rather than to hold any exchanges or Special Drawing Rights. The result would be a sharp fall in the total of generally acceptable monetary reserves in spite of any conceivable increase in the amount of 'paper gold'. Since all exchanges in turn would come under suspicion at one time or other, and most countries would come to distrust each other, the maximum amount of Special Drawing Rights that would be created would be much lower under floating exchanges than under fixed parities. For that maximum would surely have to bear some vague psychological relationship to the total of gold plus hard currencies that must be the ultimate backing of 'paper gold', which need not be redeemed and would not be wanted by any Government once it ceases to be certain that other Governments would readily accept it instead of insisting on payment in gold or hard currencies. The intrinsic value of the 'paper gold' might then decline to the price paid by paper mills for high-quality paper for re-pulping, which is 50 shillings per ton at the time of writing, but might well rise to £3, £4, and even higher as a result of the inflation that 'paper gold' will help to generate.

Of course the dream of the 'dollar lobby' in Washington is to put the world on the dollar standard under which every country other than the United States would find itself to be out of step whenever excessive domestic expansion in the United States or over-exporting of American capital by the United States would weaken the dollar. The remedy prescribed for such occasion would be a revaluation of all currencies whenever they become stronger than the dollar, so as to enable the United States to avoid a devaluation of the dollar. It remains to be seen, however, whether the world could be persuaded to adopt that solution.

CHAPTER TWENTY

Doing the Right Thing in the Wrong Way

IT was argued in the last chapter that a substantial increase in the American price of gold would be essential in order to ensure a satisfactory operation of the Bretton Woods system. As things appear at the time of writing, however, the chances of a major devaluation of the dollar are extremely remote. The overwhelming majority of American expert opinion, political opinion and public opinion is firmly against it. The maintenance of the official price of gold at $35 has come to be regarded as a matter of national honour and prestige. This in spite of the fact that the older generation still remember the increase in the price of gold from $20.19 to $35 in 1934. Nobody has ever held that devaluation against the American nation or against the Roosevelt administration. In fact the dollar came to command infinitely higher prestige immediately after its devaluation and during most of the time ever since than it had before its devaluation.

Moreover, those who are opposed to a devaluation on ethical grounds, because they feel that it would be a breach of faith, ought to be reminded that in 1934 the United States committed an act which constituted an incomparably graver breach of faith than the devaluation of the dollar. Congress passed legislation repudiating the clauses embodied in innumerable loan contracts guaranteeing the gold value of the dollar liabilities by stipulating that the borrowers – including the United States Government itself – must pay interest and principal in 'gold dollars of the present weight and fineness'. Yet American national honour and prestige survived that flagrant act of repudiation of a legal obligation, because everybody assumed that, unlike some other Governments, the United States Government did not intend to make a habit of such repudiations and had only resorted to it – and to the devaluation of the dollar – in extreme emergency. It is assumed that such acts would not be repeated lightly, that they would only be resorted to in situations when the alternative would be infinitely worse – as indeed it would have been in 1934.

It is of course arguable that the present situation bears no comparison with the series of grave crises and with the intractable deflationary depression of the mid-thirties, which had threatened the very foundations of the American economy and of world economy. But the possibility of the development of a similarly grave crisis as a result of the stubborn refusal of the United States to raise the price of gold must be faced. A major emergency comparable with that of the 'thirties might easily arise either as a result of a sharp contraction in world trade through the adoption of floating exchanges or as a result of the self-aggravating effect of excessive deflationary measures that might be resorted to in defence of the existing parities. It would be a matter of statesmanlike wisdom to devalue the dollar in good time for the sake of averting such a disaster instead of making it a point of honour to defer the only effective solution until it has to be adopted as a result of a catastrophic crisis.

The choice is not between devaluing or not devaluing but between devaluing to prevent a disaster or devaluing as a result of a disaster. If the United States were to delay devaluation until it becomes inevitable, it would pay a very heavy price for the luxury of false pride. It is certainly not worth while to pay such a price for the sake of deferring the inevitable by a few years.

Americans are understandably reluctant to devalue 'in cold blood'. There must be a first-rate crisis for them to feel justified before themselves and before the world to devalue. Having regard to what is at stake, such considerations ought to be set aside. The risk involved in the prolonged stubborn defence of the present dollar–gold parity is in no way inferior to the risk

President Roosevelt would have taken in 1933–34 if he had used up the gold reserve in an effort to defer the moment when he would have had to face realities. The present Washington administration should not be too proud to devalue in good time.

In two important respects it is now infinitely more dangerous to risk the recurrence of mass unemployment than it was in the 'thirties, when the alternative system to capitalism offered by the practical experience under Communism in Soviet Russia had but little attraction for working classes outside that country. Even the unemployed in capitalist countries were much better off than the starving workers and peasants in the Soviet Union. But meanwhile productivity and the standard of living in the U.S.S.R. have risen considerably. Having regard to this, mass-unemployment in the United States and in other Western countries today would swell the ranks of Communist parties. It might easily tip the balance in favour of adopting a Communist regime in countries which have already large Communist parties, such as France and Italy, and also in undeveloped countries such as India.

An even graver danger is the possibility that mass unemployment today would lead to the eruption of mass violence to an extent compared with which riots experienced in the United States and other countries during recent years would fade into insignificance. In the 'thirties the millions of unemployed in the United States, Britain and other countries submitted to their fate with a passive resignation. Today in similar conditions they would be erecting barricades and would be looting or burning down prosperous residential and business districts.

Apart from any other consideration, the United States has already actually committed an act which is at least as flagrant a breach of faith as a devaluation of the dollar would be. The usual answer to the main argument against the devaluation, that it would amount to a breach of trust towards those non-residents who have confidence in the dollar and in 'no devaluation' pledges by the United States, is that the *de facto* blocking of those official dollar reserves as an alternative to devaluation constitutes a comparable breach of faith. Although technically foreign official holders of dollar balances are still entitled to withdraw them in the form of gold at the official price, since the crisis of March 1968 they have been under the impression that if they insisted on their rights their balances would have to be officially blocked. Although exceptions are made in certain cases, for all practical purposes the dollar is inconvertible. Naturally enough foreign Central Banks and Governments prefer to keep up the fiction that the dollars they hold are convertible, so they abstain from insisting on their right, in the full knowledge that it would be useless to do so.

The stubborn rigidity of the defence of the dollar at its present gold parity was relaxed somewhat when in March 1968 the United States authorities and other participants in the Gold Pool decided that the support of the free market price of gold abroad at $35 an ounce should be discontinued. Had they taken this decision earlier they would have saved billions of dollars of monetary gold stocks which they had lost in a futile attempt to bolster up the free market price of gold by supplying speculators and hoarders with all the gold they wanted at $35. Under the new system the fluctuating free market price of gold was higher for some time than the official price. The United States authorities are now just as stubborn in defending the artificial official price as they had been in keeping down the free market price.

Why is it that Presidents Johnson and Nixon have been so much more stubborn in facing the realities of the situation than President Roosevelt had been? Of course those realities are much less obvious today than they were in 1933–34. There is as yet no mass unemployment in the United States in consequence of the prolonged defence of the old parity. Besides, even amidst the crises of the 'thirties neither the United States Government nor the British Government dared to devalue by one swift deliberate stroke. They preferred to discontinue supporting their respective currencies at gold export point by the sale of gold at its official price, and allowed the dollar and sterling to depreciate on the initiative of the foreign exchange market.

It seems at the time of writing that history might well repeat itself, because the only way in which an increase in the official dollar price of gold might become politically practicable would be through a depreciation of the dollar, to be brought about through the adoption of floating exchanges instead of facing a straight devaluation.

This was exactly what actually happened in respect of the revaluation of the D. mark in October 1969. Instead of changing its official parity straight away the West German authorities preferred to allow it to appreciate in a free market, assisting in the process through official sales of dollars.

Needless to say the German decision to embark on an experiment with floating exchanges, even temporarily and with the declared intention of restoring fixed parities at the earliest possible moment, was received with enthusiasm in the camp of supporters of the floating system. It was widely welcomed as an important precedent, although it was quite obvious that the circumstances in which the German Government resorted to that system were quite special. The Kiesinger regime did not want to revalue on the eve of the election. The political interregnum between the election and the change of Government made it impossible for the victorious party to carry out its intention to revalue the D. mark immediately. The adoption of the floating system on the eve of the election until after the election and after the change of Government was a necessary evil.

In any case there is a world of difference between the adoption of a floating system for a strong currency and its adoption for a weak currency. The authorities can quite easily control the rate and maximum extent of an appreciation of a strong currency and can prevent it from getting out of hand. Even the most sanguine speculators did not expect a revaluation of the D. mark by more than 10 per cent, and most of them put their expectations much lower. This alone set a natural limit to the speculative rise in the uncontrolled D. mark. The exceptionally large size of speculative long positions necessarily meant heavy profit-taking realisations as and when the rate was approaching the level at which the majority of operators deemed it advisable to get out. There was also the possibility of a resumption of the suspended issuing activity in D. mark Euro-bonds soon after revaluation, to offset the effect of the German export surplus even before it becomes reduced as a result of the revaluation. Because of all these considerations, the extent to which the unpegged D. mark was floating towards what was regarded as its equilibrium level was very slow, hesitant and quite inadequate. It had to be stepped up by artificial means, through official sales of dollars in addition to sales arising through the liquidation of long positions by speculators.

In spite of these considerations, the advocates of floating exchanges were jubilant. *The Economist* triumphantly informed its readers that 'a process of economic education has been set afoot which is likely to lead towards wider and wiser views of more flexible exchange rates in the future. . . . A start towards thinking about flexibility has been made.'

Those who are unenthusiastic about the adoption of floating exchanges as a permanent solution, but feel that its adoption would be justified for the limited purpose of adjusting parities, imagine that after a period of wild if temporary fluctuations the exchange rate would in fact eventually settle down at their equilibrium levels at which they could then be restabilised. It is very tempting for those of us who hold strong views about the need for raising the American price of gold and for an all-round realignment of parities to adopt the line that if exchanges were unpegged with the limited purpose of giving them a chance to depreciate or appreciate to the required extent, the resulting temporary chaos might be a price well worth paying for the sake of the benefits derived from restabilisation at the correct parities.

Those who are in favour of higher gold prices, but reject the superstition that freely fluctuating exchanges would float to their equilibrium levels, could argue that through the adoption of this strategy the right thing would happen for the wrong reason and in the wrong way. Since the United States Government and other Governments stubbornly refused to adjust their parities by deliberate action, it is tempting to argue that the next best thing would be to resort to the face-saving device of allowing the exchanges to find their new parities.

We saw in earlier chapters, however, how utterly false the belief is that if the exchanges are allowed to take care of themselves they would settle down eventually at their trade equilibrium levels. Speculative and other influences would produce entirely fortuitous rates unrelated to their equilibrium level, and exaggerated exchange movement would tend to bring about basic changes in the equilibrium levels. Nor is there any reason to assume that the rates would remain in the vicinity of their new equilibrium levels for any considerable length of time. Quite conceivably the pattern of parities that would emerge from the chaos after the exchanges are re-stabilised might be even more out of equilibrium than the existing pattern of parities.

Moreover during the period of transition the chaotic conditions created by wildly fluctuating exchanges are liable to cause irreparable harm. They might lead to another world slump with incalculable consequences. They would be certain to lead to a revival of economic nationalism. There would be competitive depreciation races similar to those experienced in the 'thirties and a return to the 'beggar-my-neighbour' policy of the bad old days. The free world would become dangerously disunited at a time when its unity would be increasingly essential in face of the growing threat of Communist-imperialist aggression.

Perhaps it would be worth while to recall in this connection that the competitive depreciation race between Britain and the United States during the 'thirties degenerated at times into financial warfare between the two Anglo-Saxon countries. An attempt to bring the conflict to an end by summoning a world economic conference in London in 1933 failed completely and the conflict continued until the conclusion of the Tripartite Agreement in 1936. It gave rise to much ill-feeling between London and Washington, and also between countries with floating exchanges on the one hand and the countries of the Gold Bloc on the other. It led to an upsurge of economic nationalism, higher tariffs, quotas, bilateral trading, exchange clearing, etc. It created strained relations between peace-loving nations and must have contributed to some extent at any rate towards the encouragement of aggressive Nazi policy.

After the outbreak of the Second World War the reason why President Roosevelt found it for a long time so difficult to persuade Congress to authorise financial assistance to Britain must have been to a large extent the delayed effect of the memories of Anglo-American financial warfare before 1939. It would be a matter of common sense to avoid the repetition of that history. The free world must show a united front in face of the menace of Russian and Chinese aggression. It would be foolish to forget the costly lesson taught in the 'thirties when the disruption of the united front between democratic nations for the sake of securing advantages at each other's expense by means of competitive currency depreciation gave Hitler his opportunity to organise Germany for a war of world conquest.

Is it really necessary to await a major crisis and the advent of prolonged chaotic conditions before the United States Government resorts to the inevitable solution of adapting the official price of gold to realities? If it was justified to resort to such a measure in order to emerge from the crisis of the 'thirties, surely it is equally justified to resort to it in order to avoid the recurrence of such a crisis in the 'seventies. Indeed the reasons why common sense should be made to prevail are even weightier today than they were in the 'thirties. Ill-advised monetary policy then prepared the way for Nazi military victory. Ill-advised monetary policy now, in addition to preparing the way for military victory of Communist aggressors, would greatly assist them in achieving a bloodless victory without running the risk of a military defeat.

It is understandable if those in sympathy with the Communist system favour monetary policies which would lead to a victory for that system without having to risk a major war. It is much more difficult to understand why academic and political quarters hostile to Communism are short-sighted enough to play into the hands of the Communists. They fail to realise that the policy of stubborn defence of parities, and the policy of abandoning those parities altogether, equally endanger the existence of the democratic way of life.

President Nixon, in his message to Congress on February 18, condemned the American-invented Bretton Woods system as being too rigid, forcing countries 'to adopt internal economic policies, such as excessive rates of inflation or unemployment, which conflict with their national economic and social objectives. Both approaches have been adopted all too frequently in the past.' Alas, they have been adopted in the wrong sense. Countries such as the United States and Britain, which ought to have been deflating to eliminate the deficits on their balance of payments, have been inflating instead, while countries such as Germany (until 1969) and France (until 1968), which ought to have been inflating to reduce their export surpluses, have been deflating. Evidently it is not the system that is wrong but its application.

Anyhow, if President Nixon is in favour of relaxing the rigidity of parities, then flexibility, like charity, should begin at home. Why not set an example by abandoning the rigid defence of the unrealistic dollar–gold parity?

APPENDIX

Why are U.K. Firms forbidden to Hedge?

WHETHER we like it or not, the world seems to be moving towards a higher degree of flexibility of exchange rates. Business firms will have to reckon with the possibility of wider and more frequent changes in exchange rates. It is to their interests to safeguard themselves against risks of losses arising from such changes.

Such risks may assume one of two forms. There are direct and definite risks arising from a definite claim or liability in terms of a foreign currency the value of which might go up or down by the time payment is due to be received or made. Under existing regulations there is nothing to prevent British firms from covering such risks by means of a forward exchange contract. Importers are entitled to buy in advance from their banks the foreign exchange they will need, up to the statutory time limit determined by the exchange control regulations, and the banks will deliver the foreign currency on the day when the payment falls due. Exporters are entitled to sell in advance to their banks the proceeds of their sales invoiced in terms of foreign currencies.

The transaction may be costly to importers and profitable to exporters if the forward exchanges in question are at a big premium. It may be profitable to importers and costly to exporters if the forward exchanges in question are at a big discount. What matters is that firms are at liberty to insure themselves against losses arising from transactions involving a definite contractual claim or liability in terms of a foreign currency.

There are, however, different types of exchange risks to which industrial and commercial firms are exposed, against which firms in the U.K. are not permitted under existing exchange control regulations to insure themselves. They are not allowed to engage in forward exchange transactions to safeguard themselves against a fall in the sterling value of their investments abroad that might result from a depreciation of the currency of the country in which they have invested. And they are not allowed to engage in forward exchange transactions to safeguard themselves against a fall in the sterling prices of their stocks of imported goods that might result from a depreciation of the currency of the exporting country. In other words, while they are free to *cover* direct and definite exchange risks, they are forbidden to *hedge* against indirect and indefinite exchange risks, even though the latter are none the less real for being indirect and indefinite.

The basic theoretical, practical and legal difference between *covering* and *hedging* is not realised sufficiently. Most economists use the two terms indiscriminately. Our first task is, therefore, to make the difference quite clear.

As already remarked above, covering forward exchange operations aim at safeguarding ourselves against losses incurred through changes in exchange rates on payments of definite amounts in a foreign currency due to be made or received on a definite date. The extent of the losses against which we want to safeguard ourselves is proportionate to the change in the exchange rate that might occur by the time the payment becomes due.

Forward exchange operations for hedging purposes aim at safeguarding ourselves against indirect and indefinite losses through changes in exchange rates, incurred through their indirect effect on the value of our investments or our inventories. The two types of hedging differ from each other considerably and must be examined separately.

A typical instance of investment hedging, encountered all too frequently during the 'sixties, is forward selling of sterling by American firms which own branches or subsidiaries in the U.K. whenever they expect, rightly or wrongly, that sterling might be devalued. 'The Great West Road (a district where many American factories are situated) is selling sterling' is an expression that was frequently encountered in financial columns and in conversations between foreign exchange dealers whenever sterling was under pressure. American firms with direct investments in Britain – or, for that matter, with portfolio investments consisting of shareholdings in British firms – often wanted to safeguard themselves against a depreciation of their assets in terms of dollars that would occur through a devaluation of sterling. To that end they sold sterling forward on the assumption that the profit they would make on that operation if sterling should be devalued would compensate them for the depreciation of their sterling investments in terms of dollars.

Such operations have inevitably a speculative element. While covering of claims or liabilities with the aid of forward exchange transactions means the *closing* of an open position, hedging against losses on an investment means *creating* an open position. In my *Textbook on Foreign Exchange* I define hedging as 'taking a speculative risk in order to offset a bigger speculative risk in the opposite sense'.

The American firms which created a short position of sterling exposed themselves to a speculative loss – albeit a limited one and a calculable one – through a recovery of sterling. But they deemed it worth while to run that moderate risk for the sake of safeguarding themselves against a much more substantial loss through the effect of a devaluation of sterling on the dollar value of their sterling assets. The extent of that loss was not a calculable one, not only because it was impossible to foresee the extent of a devaluation if it should occur, but also because the effect of a devaluation on the dollar value of American sterling investments was no matter of simple arithmetic.

Quite possibly the sterling value of those investments might increase as a result of the devaluation – indeed in the long run it was bound to increase through the gradual adjustment of British prices and values to the reduced international value of sterling and through the improvement of trading prospects of the U.K. subsidiary as a result of the devaluation. But the immediate adverse effect was liable to be substantial, and it was a legitimate operation to safeguard against such losses through selling sterling forward.

Owing to the large and increasing amount of American and other foreign investments in British industries, the volume of such hedging operations was very considerable whenever sterling was under a cloud. It was, of course, greatly encouraged by the official support of forward sterling at an artificial level between 1964 and 1967, which reduced to a minimum the 'insurance premium' paid by hedgers in the form of the premium on forward dollars.

The other type of hedging is the forward sale of the currency of the exporting country by holders of imported goods – merchants dealing in imported goods or manufacturers having stocks of imported raw materials, semi-products or even equipment. If these goods are invoiced in terms of the currency of the exporting country, there is no need to hedge against its devaluation until the account is settled, for the depreciation of that currency would compensate, and more than compensate, the holders of imported goods for the effect of that depreciation on the prices of these goods in terms of their own currency. But if the goods are invoiced in terms of their own currency or in terms of a third currency, or even if they are invoiced in terms of the exporter's currency but the importers still hold some of the imported goods after they have settled their accounts, they are exposed to losses through a fall in the prices of their stocks of imported goods caused by a devaluation of the exporters' currency.

To take a concrete example, a substantial devaluation of sterling would reduce materially the dollar prices of British cars imported by American dealers. If the cars are invoiced in sterling the American buyers need not worry about it unless they still have unsold imported cars after they have paid their sterling debt to the exporters or to the bank financing the transaction. But if they have unsold cars at that stage, or if the cars were invoiced in dollars, they are exposed to losses through reductions in the dollar prices of imported cars. Unless they reduce their dollar prices following on a devaluation of sterling, their rivals who would import British cars after the devaluation would be in a position to undersell them. They would feel forced, therefore, to reduce their prices, thereby incurring losses or at any rate reducing their profit margins.

American and other importers of British and Sterling Area goods safeguarded themselves against that risk by selling sterling forward whenever they suspected that there might be a devaluation in the not too distant future. Such operations greatly increased the selling pressure on forward sterling on such occasions.

Of course, sterling was not the only devaluation-prone currency. British investors abroad and British holders of imported stocks of goods were also exposed to risks similar to those described above. The difference between their position and that of American firms was that while the latter were free to safeguard themselves against such risks, U.K. firms were forbidden to do so under exchange control regulations. This may sound quite incredible. For hedging by British firms would have meant buying of forward sterling, and such operations would have meant much-needed support to sterling. But the British authorities in their wisdom prevented, and are still preventing, British residents from supporting sterling by engaging in hedging operations.

Possibly, until 1968 the extent to which British firms would have hedged even if they had been at liberty to do so would have been moderate. For sterling was all too frequently under suspicion, even after its devaluation in 1967, so that most British investors abroad and holders of imported goods would have preferred to abstain from selling forward the currency of their investment or the currency of the exporters. They might have hedged, however, against currencies which were even more devaluation-prone than sterling. None of the important currencies belonged to that category.

But since May 1968 there has been a distinct possibility of a devaluation of the French franc in terms of sterling. Many firms holding direct investments in France and holders of inventories of goods imported from France would have liked to safeguard themselves against the risk of losses through such a devaluation. But under the existing exchange regulations they were not allowed to hedge against that risk. At the beginning of 1970 sterling became, temporarily at any rate, a strong currency, so that the possibility of its appreciation in terms of other currencies gave rise to a risk of losses on investments and on imports.

The handicap imposed on British firms investing abroad or holding imported goods by preventing them from safeguarding their legitimate interests is liable to increase in importance as a result of an increase in the flexibility of exchange rates. Whatever form that increase may assume, British firms will be exposed to many more risks against which they are unable to hedge. They are liable to suffer many more losses in circumstances similar to those suffered as a result of the devaluation of the franc.

Is it not high time for the Treasury and the Bank of England to reconsider their attitude towards hedging? That attitude has been in any case utterly unreasonable, and it is impossible to think of a single valid argument in its favour. But so long as sterling was the only devaluation-prone major currency and pressure against it was unilateral, the handicap imposed on British industry and trade by this ban on hedging was relatively moderate. Now that the cat is liable to jump either way, the disadvantages of that handicap could assume considerable proportions. As the 'English disease' is spreading over other industrial countries, any country is liable to become devaluation-prone. We must remember that the franc, which was the strongest currency until May 1968, became the weakest currency within weeks and remained the weakest currency for 18 months.

To show the absurdity of the official attitude, let it be sufficient to quote a single instance. The price of imported French wines in Britain is naturally liable to be affected by changes in the sterling–franc rate. When sterling was devalued in terms of francs in 1967 their prices were raised. When the franc was devalued in terms of sterling two years later their prices were or are reduced – though admittedly not quite so fast as the increases following on the devaluation of sterling.

So U.K. wine merchants are exposed to risks through changes in the sterling–franc rate. They are at liberty to cover the risk of a loss through a devaluation of sterling if the wines are invoiced in francs, by buying francs for forward delivery. But they are prevented from covering a loss through a devaluation of the franc as a result of which they are compelled to lower the prices of their wines imported and paid for before the devaluation. They could easily do so by the simple expedient of selling francs forward when they expect a devaluation of the franc. It would be a legitimate transaction because they have a genuine interest to protect. But they are not entitled to protect it.

When I asked for an official explanation of the ban on hedging transactions, I was told that under the established rule only contractual claims or liabilities could be covered, and no contractual claims or liabilities are involved in the holding of foreign investments or of imported goods. If a U.K. investor in a foreign country chooses to sell his investment and payment is due at a future date, he is entitled to sell the proceeds forward. But if he wants to retain his investment he is not permitted to safeguard himself against losses through a devaluation of the country in which he has invested.

No conceivable public interest is involved in the adoption and maintenance of this strange rule which does not exist in some other advanced countries. Quite the contrary, as already said, by preventing firms from hedging against their foreign investments and against their inventories in imported goods, the authorities prevent them supporting sterling. While foreign investors in Britain and foreign importers of British or Sterling Area goods are free to increase the pressure on sterling by hedging against their investments or inventories, their British opposite numbers are forbidden to help sterling.

The Government laid down the rule that there must be a contractual claim or liability to make a foreign exchange operation by a

U.K. resident permissible. This rule does not form part of the Ten Commandments or of the Laws of the Medes and Persians. It is a man-made rule which could be altered by a stroke of the pen, without even having to amend any existing legislation. It is sheer boneheaded bureaucracy that has upheld it and is still upholding it regardless of the growing strength of the case for its removal. The bureaucrats of Whitehall and Threadneedle Street feel bound by the rule they themselves or their predecessors in office had laid down.

Before very long we are liable to enter a period of frequent and substantial changes of exchange parities and exchange rates. American, German, Japanese industrial and commercial firms are in a position to take decisions they deem necessary in order to safeguard their legitimate interests against the effects of such changes on the value of their assets – but industrial and commercial firms in the U.K. are prevented from doing so.

If a British manufacturer deems it necessary to accumulate a large inventory in imported raw materials or semi-products and the currency of the exporting country is devaluation-prone, he has to choose between deferring the purchase of his much-needed materials until after the devaluation – which might never happen – and running the risk of placing himself at a disadvantage if his rival should purchase the materials after the devaluation. It would be a simple solution if he were permitted – as his foreign rivals are permitted – to hedge against his inventory by selling forward the currency of the exporting country. If he is prevented from doing so and prefers to postpone his purchase beyond immediate requirements, and if in the absence of a devaluation of the exporter's currency the prices of the raw materials should increase, he would suffer a loss.

There are quite enough unavoidable risks businessmen have to face nowadays against which it is impossible to hedge. But the British authorities go out of their way to increase their number by preventing hedging operations in circumstances in which they might provide the solution of the problem. In doing so they don't even serve their own broader interests. For, during a period of exchange fluctuations we are likely to experience, sterling will need every support it can obtain. Yet the British authorities forgo deliberately support that would be forthcoming freely if U.K. residents were allowed to hedge against the devaluation of other currencies.

There is another aspect of the problem. Decisions whether to invest abroad depend on a wide variety of considerations, and official decisions whether to encourage or discourage such investment also depend on a wide variety of considerations. But U.K. investments abroad that would suit the interests of the firms and would also be viewed with favour by the British authorities are discouraged by the authorities by depriving the firms of the opportunity to safeguard their investments against the risk of a loss through a devaluation of the currency of the country in which they would invest become devaluation-prone.

It is true, as was pointed out in Chapter 13, that as a result of an adoption of floating exchanges – or of an increase in the flexibility of exchange rates through the adoption of one of the alternative systems to that end – forward exchange facilities are liable to become scarce and costly. But that is no reason for reserving them for those who want to use them for covering, while continuing to prevent U.K. firms from hedging against their increased risks. In any case firms outside the U.K. would increase their demands for forward exchange facilities for hedging purposes. To deprive U.K. firms of the means of safeguarding themselves against their increased risks would inflict on them unnecessary disadvantages through an ill-advised exchange control regulation.

Bibliography

ASCHINGER, F. E., 'Flexible Wechselkurse: eine Scheinlösung', *Die Weltwoche* (Zürich), 31 Jan 1969.

BALDWIN, R. E. (ed.), *Trade Growth and the Balance of Payments* (Chicago, 1966).

CASSEL, GUSTAV, *Money and Foreign Exchange after 1914* (London, 1922).

COOPER, R. N. (ed.), *International Finance* (Harmondsworth, 1969).

EINZIG, PAUL, *The History of Foreign Exchange*, 2nd ed. (London, 1970).

——, *A Dynamic Theory of Forward Exchange*, 2nd ed. (London, 1967).

——, *The Euro-Dollar System*, 4th ed. (London, 1970).

——, *A Textbook on Foreign Exchange*, 2nd ed. (London, 1969).

——, *Foreign Exchange Crises*, 2nd ed. (London, 1970).

——, *Leads and Lags* (London, 1968).

——, *Decline and Fall? Britain's Crisis in the Sixties* (London, 1969).

——, *The Euro-Bond Market*, 2nd ed. (London, 1969).

FRIEDMAN, MILTON, *Essays in Positive Economics* (Chicago, 1953).

GRUBEL, HERBERT G. (ed.), *World Monetary Reform* (London, 1964).

HABERLET, GOTTFRIED, *Money in the International Economy* (London, 1965).

HAHN, L. ALBERT, 'Geld ohne Gold', *Neue Zürcher Zeitung*, 4, 6 and 7 Aug 1968.

HALM, GEORGE N., *The 'Band' Proposal of Permissible Exchange Rate Variations* (Princeton, 1965).

HARROD, SIR ROY, *Reforming the World's Money* (London, 1965).

JOHNSON, H. G., and NASH, JOHN E., *The U.K. and Floating Exchanges* (London, 1969).

LANYI, ANTHONY, *The Case for Floating Exchange Rates Reconsidered* (Princeton, 1969).

LEAGUE OF NATIONS, *International Currency Experience: Lessons of the Inter-War Period*, ed. Ragnar Nurkse (Geneva, 1944).

MACHLUP, FRITZ, *Plans for Reform of the International Monetary System* (Princeton, 1962).

——, *International Monetary Economics* (London, 1966).

——(ed.), *Maintaining and Restoring Balance in International Payment* (Princeton, 1966).

MELLISH, C. HARTLEY, and HAWKINS, ROBERT C., *The Stability of Flexible Exchanges: The Canadian Experience* (New York, 1968).

MORGAN, E. V., 'The Theory of Flexible Exchange Rates', *American Economic Review* (June 1955).

Mundell, A., 'Problems of Monetary Management and Exchange Rate Policy in Canada', *National Banking Review* (Sep 1964).

Powell, Enoch, *Exchange Rates and Liquidity* (London, 1967).

Powrie, T. L., 'Short-term Capital Movements and the Flexible Canadian Exchange Rate', *Canadian Journal of Economic and Political Science* (Feb 1964).

Robbins, Lord, 'The International Monetary Problem', *Journal of Political Economy* (July–Aug 1968).

Romberg, Rudolf, 'A Model of the Canadian Economy under Fixed and Fluctuating Exchange Rates', *Journal of Political Economy* (Feb 1964).

Rosenbluth, G., 'Changes in Canadian Sensitivity to United States Business Fluctuations', *Canadian Journal of Economic and Political Science* (Nov 1957).

Sedillot, René, *Du franc Bonaparte au franc de Gaulle* (Paris, 1960).

Shepherd, Sidney A., *Foreign Exchange in Canada: An Outline*, 3rd ed. (Toronto, 1961).

Sohmen, Egon, *Flexible Exchange Rates: Theory and Controversy* (Chicago 1961).

——, *International Monetary Problems and the Foreign Exchanges* (Princeton, 1963).

Tsiang, S. C., *Fluctuating Exchange Rates in Countries with Relatively Stable Economies*, I.M.F. Staff Papers vii (New York, 1959–60).

Williamson, John H., *The Crawling Peg* (Princeton, 1966).

Wonnacott, Paul, *The Canadian Dollar, 1948–1962* (Toronto, 1965).

Yeager, Leland B., *International Monetary Relations* (New York, 1966).

Index